**Outdo, Outwit &
Outperform**

Other books available by Peter Wade:

Exciting Ephesians
I Am Not A Victim
God's Seeds of Greatness
Four Keys to Daily Positive Living
Four Keys to Prosperity
God's Secrets of Success
Positive Principles:
   Book 1—Studies in God's Positive Word

Outdo, Outwit & Outperform

Peter Wade

My thanks to...
> Vivien Wade, whose support has never wavered over a third of a century;
>
> My proofreading team: Tony Butz, Paul Kery, Gene McClarty and Vivien Wade;
>
> And supporters of this positive ministry, both in Australia and the United States, who have made this book possible.

Positive Word Ministries Inc.,
G.P.O. Box 450, Adelaide S.A. 5001, Australia.
Copyright © 1995 Peter Wade
ISBN 0 909362 24 6
All rights reserved
Typeset by Positive Word Ministries Inc.
Printed by Australian Print Group, Maryborough VIC 3465

The Bible text in this publication, except where otherwise indicated, is from the New International Version (NIV). Copyright © 1973, 1978, 1984 by International Bible Society. Used by permission.

Contents

    First Words 7
1. How to Outdo the Law of Averages 9
2. How to Outwit Murphy's Law 19
3. How to Outperform the Peter Principle .. 29
4. How to Have God as Your Partner 37
5. How to Win With God's Weapons 46
6. How to Have a Successful Year 54
7. How to Keep Your Head Out of a Lion's Mouth 62

8	How to Kill the Giants In Your Life	70
9	How to Handle Discouragement	79
10	How to Survive a Catastrophe	88
	Last Words	96

First Words

Christianity was always intended to be a practical way of life, rather than a ritualistic religion. Its founder made this clear in the parable of the house built upon the rock: "Therefore everyone who hears these words of mine and puts them into practice is like a wise man who built his house on the rock" (Matthew 7:24 NIV). The apostle Paul had two main sections in each epistle—doctrine and deed. For example, he urged the Ephesians believers "to live a life worthy of the calling you have received" (Ephesians 4:1). He also urged the Philippian believers to "continue to work out [carry out to its completion] your salvation..., for it is God who works in you..." (Philippians 2:12–13).

In addition, James, the Lord's brother, also made it clear in his epistle that believers should "...humbly accept the word planted in you, which can save you. Do not merely listen to the word, and so deceive yourselves. Do what it says" (James 1:21-22).

In this book I am sharing with you ten "How to..." chapters to help you to live out the Christ life in you. These teachings are based upon the same positive and positional truths I have explored in other writings. They were first given to a fellowship of believers, of whom the majority were business men and women. At that time the emphasis was on encouraging them to take the positive Word of God into their business life and apply it to their needs in that area. Now that I committed these teachings to paper, I am convinced that the truths they contain are applicable to all Christian believers in most of life's situations.

Here are intensely practical ways to fully express the Christ within you—in your personal life, your family or home life, and in your business life. The Word works whenever you apply it. I trust that these ten chapters will enourage you to trust in and apply God's Word today and all your tomorrows.

Chapter One

How to Outdo the Law of Averages

*B*enjamin Disraeli said, "There are three kinds of lies: lies, damn lies and statistics." It seems that the media are constantly feeding us with statistics. One in four people are going to get this or one in five people have got that. They tell us that one in three marriages are going to end in divorce. They say that the average Australian consumes "x" litres of wine each year or the average Australian drinks so much tea a year. The media are using what is called the law of averages. The average is the arithmetical mean, established by adding a set of values and dividing the total by the number of items. It represents the middle or median point in a range of given values. In these days most database programs provide the means to establish the average of almost everything. Many people believe what the media says, and they believe the law of averages. But should you, as a Christian, believe it?

"You are still worldly. For since there is jealousy and quarreling among you, are you not worldly? Are you not acting like mere men?" (I Corinthians 3:3 NIV). Other translations render the word "worldly" as "carnal" (KJV) or "sense governed". The statement concerns Christians whose actions are governed by the information coming to them via the five senses. They are acting "like mere men", or "mere humans" as I should render it these days. They are acting just like everyone else in the world, hence the translation "worldly".

I am concerned about the law of averages because I feel it has two inherent dangers. One is that it encourages people to pessimism and soon becomes fatalism, where they think that certain events must happen. For example, if our marriage happens to be marriage number three then I have an unavoidable appointment at the divorce court. I had better prepare a pre-nuptial agreement! The law of averages may be a handy statistical device but it is only that. The average certainly cannot be guaranteed at the individual level.

The second inherent danger is that people could conclude that perhaps they are just average people. If the average Australian drinks x cups of tea a year, and I too drink about x cups, then I'm just an average person. The same comparisons are made about salaries, values of houses, makes of car and so forth. I believe the Bible is quite clear that those who belong to God's forever family are anything but average.

They are more than conquerors, they are blessed with Heaven's best, they are victors!

I have a distinct dislike for the law of averages, because I believe it is contrary to what God says about us in His Word. We must come to the place where we ask, "Am I a statistic or am I a person?" "Am I an average person or am I a child of God?" The two terms are mutually exclusive. Statistics do teach us certain things. For example, we know that one in five people in Australia believe in God and believe the Bible to be the Word of God, but they do not go to church. These statistics are helpful so long as we do not label people on that basis. And while one in three marriages might end in divorce nationally, why should one in three marriages in your fellowship end in divorce, just because of the law of averages? So let's learn how to outdo the law of averages.

God's answers to Moses

I have taken as illustrations three people in the Bible who thought they were average or less. We will look at these examples and see how God encouraged them to change their thinking and to outdo their belief in the law of averages.

The first person is Moses, as recorded in the book of Exodus. Let's see what Moses has to say about himself and how God answered him. In Exodus chapter 3 Moses had left Pharaoh's house and had become a shepherd in the wilderness. God came to Moses one day and told him he was needed to lead the nation of Israel out of their bondage. "But Moses said to God, 'Who am I, that I should go to Pharaoh and bring the Israelites out of Egypt?'" (Exodus 3:11 NIV). Moses said, in effect, that he was just keeping sheep for his father-in-law Jethro. He felt that God did not want a shepherd for this job but somebody with a little panache, somebody with the latest fashion suit, somebody who was not wanted by the law of the land. Moses saw himself as below average. How did God answer him?

"And God said, 'I will be with you. And this will be the sign to you that it is I who have sent you: When you have brought the people out of Egypt, you will worship God on this mountain.'" (Exodus 3:12). "Certainly I will be with thee" (KJV)—what more could you want? Notice that God did not even comment on Moses' objection. He simply stated the obvious, "I will be with you". That is a great key to outdoing the law of averages: you cannot be just average if God is with you. You and God are a majority. You are no longer just an average person, you're somebody special.

There was much discussion as Moses tried to prove to God that he really was just an average man and not up to the task. "Moses answered, "What if they do not believe me or listen to me and say, 'The Lord did not appear to you'?" (Exodus 4:1). Moses' argument was that they would not believe a shepherd. He had not had contact with the Israelites for a number of years. How did God answer this objection? The first time God answered Moses was with the truth of His presence; this time he answers him with the truth of His power. "Then the Lord said to him, 'What is that in your hand?' 'A staff,' he replied. The Lord said, 'Throw it on the ground.' Moses threw it on the ground and it became a snake, and he ran from it" (Exodus 4:2-3). I think I would have done the same! That was something quite amazing, for Moses to have a wooden staff in his hand, and then to throw it on the ground and watch it become a snake. That clearly shows the power of God in operation. And then I love this next bit, for I'm certain the Lord has a sense of humour.

"Then the Lord said to him, 'Reach out your hand and take it by the tail.'" (Exodus 4:4a). I think that some of the story is missing here, because Moses probably turned around and said, "You've got to be kidding, Lord!" It's easy enough to have a staff in your hand and to throw it down, and it becomes a serpent. That I could handle, just as long as I was a fair distance away from the snake, but to bend down and pick it up—now that's another story! But Moses did it. "So Moses reached out and took hold of the snake and it turned back into a staff in his hand. 'This,' said the Lord, 'is so that they may believe that the Lord, the God of their fathers—the God of Abraham, the God of Isaac and the God of Jacob—has appeared to you.'" (Exodus 4:4b-5).

So God gave Moses a sign that he could use when he went to the people of Israel and said that God had spoken to him. Whenever he wanted to prove that it was true, he would just throw the old staff down. I reckon he became good at this after a while, and he probably enjoyed watching the response on people's faces when he threw the staff down and it became a snake and when he picked up the snake it became a staff again.

And just in case, God gave him another two signs. "Then the Lord said, 'Put your hand inside your cloak.' So Moses put his hand into his cloak, and when he took it out, it was leprous, like snow. 'Now put it back into your cloak,' he said. So Moses put his hand back into his cloak, and when he took it out, it was restored, like the rest of his flesh. Then the Lord said, 'If they do not believe you or pay attention to the first miraculous sign, they may believe the second. But if they do not believe these two signs or listen to you, take some water from the Nile and pour it on the dry ground. The water you take from the river will become blood on the ground.'" (Exodus 4:6-9).

These three manifestations of God's power were not only signs to the nation of Israel but they were also God's sign to Moses that he was not just an average person. Moses was given God's power and he could use it whenever he willed to do so. There's a natural part in every miracle and there is a divine part. The natural part was to throw the staff on the ground. Anybody can do that. The natural part was to put his hand inside his coat. Anybody can do that. The natural part was to get some water out of the river. Anybody can do that. When man does his part, then God, by that great principle of divine-human reciprocity, does His part and the miracle takes place.

God demonstrated to Moses that he was not just average, but Moses was still not fully convinced. So God in his great love and mercy listened to Moses one more time. If it had been me, I think I would have shut the door in his face by now. "Moses said to the Lord, 'O Lord, I have never been eloquent, neither in the past nor since you have spoken to your servant. I am slow of speech and tongue.'" (Exodus 4:10). "I'm slow of speech, just average. Unaccustomed as I am to public speaking..."

"The Lord said to him, 'Who gave man his mouth?

Who makes him deaf or mute? Who gives him sight or makes him blind? Is it not I, the Lord? Now go; I will help you speak and will teach you what to say.'" (Exodus 4:11-12). What is God's key here? God has pointed out the truth of His presence and the truth of His power. Now it is the truth of His proclamation. You are not average when you put the word of God on your lips, when you say what God has said about the situation. This is why I encourage people to use affirmations, because they are saying what God said. I want Christians to see that they are not just ordinary people—they are special people, sons and daughters of the living God.

God gave Moses three keys that helped him to outdo the law of averages. The first was God's presence, the second was God's power, and the third was God's proclamation. Moses learnt that he was not average, and he went on to lead the nation of Israel for forty years.

Believe you are above average

Let's go on to another incident, this time from the New Testament, "When Jesus had entered Capernaum, a centurion came to him, asking for help. 'Lord,' he said, 'my servant lies at home paralyzed and in terrible suffering.' Jesus said to him, 'I will go and heal him.' The centurion replied, 'Lord, I do not deserve to have you come under my roof...'" (Matthew 8:6-8a).

In the same incident recorded in Luke 7:6b-7a, the centurion says, "Lord, don't trouble yourself, for I do not deserve to have you come under my roof. That is why I did not even consider myself worthy to come to you." The centurion believed that he was below average, that he did not belong in that level of company. He recognised that there was something about Jesus that was at a level higher than he was at that time. I've met thousands of Christian believers and it concerns me greatly when I hear them say, "I'm not worthy of this or of that" and many even sing songs about it. If God made you worthy, you are worthy, right? If God made you above average, you are above average. If God made you His child, then you are above average.

However, while the centurion felt he was below average, he also had faith. "... 'But just say the word, and my servant will be healed. For I myself am a man under authority, with soldiers under me. I tell this one, "Go," and he goes; and that one, "Come," and he comes. I say to my servant, "Do this," and he does it.' When Jesus heard this, he was astonished and said to those following him, 'I tell you the truth, I have not found anyone in Israel with such great faith'" (Matthew 8:8b-10). What an observation about a non-Jewish person! "Then Jesus said to the centurion, 'Go! It will be done just as you believed it would.' And his servant was healed at that very hour" (Matthew 8:13).

Here is another key to outdo the law of averages—it's the key of believing. Believe that you are above average. Believe, as it says in Psalm 91:7 that though "a thousand may fall at your side, ten thousand at your right hand, ... it will not come near you". Believe that you are above average. Remember, the law of averages is merely a statistical device; it is not the gospel. Believe the Word of God, believe what God says about you. If you can believe you can go beyond the law of averages, you can be in the high bracket instead of the middle or low bracket. When you believe, you receive—and that makes the difference.

It's the contents that count

My final illustration is from the Apostle Paul. There are many more people in the Bible who felt they were less than average and God had to teach them otherwise. Paul said, "... and last of all he appeared to me also, as to one abnormally born. For I am the least of the apostles and do not even deserve to be called an apostle, because I persecuted the church of God. But by the grace of God I am what I am, and his grace to me was not without effect. No, I worked harder than all of them—yet not I, but the grace of God that was with me" (I Corinthians 15:8-10).

"I am the least of the apostles..." That's below average, isn't it? But then Paul said, and this is the key to how he outdid the law of averages, "... by the grace of God I am what I am." That is a powerful statement. I might feel myself that I am average or less than average, but that's not true because God made me what I am. He goes on to say, "I worked harder than all of them—yet not I, but the grace of God that was with me". His part was to work harder than all the apostles put together, yet it was really Paul expressing the Christ within, "the grace of God that was with me".

Paul taught the same thing in Galatians 2:20: "I have been crucified with Christ and I no longer live, but Christ lives in me. The life I live in the body, I live by faith in the Son of God, who loved me and gave himself for me." Paul was very appreciative of the fact that he was merely a container of the Christ. And because he was a container, he was giving all the credit to the contents and not to the container. When you pick a jar off the supermarket shelf, you don't usually buy it because of the jar—you buy it because of the contents. In both these passages Paul is saying that the container was not the important thing, it was the contents that counted. Because the contents were "the grace of God", "Christ living in me", then he was way above average.

I do not believe Paul spent much time going around saying he was below average. He was conscious of the fact that he had persecuted the Christians and that he had put many of them to death. But he also recognised that he was a man of God, he was a person who had God's power and God's grace and God's Son (Galatians 1:16) in his life to do a particular task, and he got on with the doing of it. So learn from these statements that since Christ is your life, then you are not average. You can tap into God's wisdom, God's love, and God's power, so what the law of averages says is true of your community does not necessarily have to be true of yourself. You are on a higher level than the law of averages.

In conclusion, remember that the law of averages is really just a statistical device, not something that is laid down to control your life. As a Christian you are living on a different plane, where God says he wants only the best for you. He has health, wealth and happiness available for you, if you will believe his Word and fulfil its conditions. I like the affirmation that says, "I am what God says I am and I can do what God says I can do." Take that as your principle and throw out the law of averages. You will make a success of life and bring glory to God. You can outdo the law of averages.

Chapter Two

How to Outwit Murphy's Law

*T*here are many times in life when things don't quite go the way you would like them to go. Have you ever just got into the bath or shower and the telephone rang? Have you ever rushed out to answer it and it was a wrong number? Have you ever washed the car and it started raining an hour later? Some people say that these incidents are an outworking of Murphy's Law. Murphy's Law is often defined this way: "If anything can go wrong, it will". There are hundreds of examples of this in daily life.

A minister attended a lecture on church growth. The lecturer met him again some months later and asked, "How is it going?" He replied, "You'll never believe it. I came to your lecture on church growth and while I was there three families left my church. I then decided to implement a program called Explosion Evangelism and it didn't even go off with a whimper. Finally I got so desperate that I phoned Dial-a-Prayer but I got the wrong number!" Murphy's Law: If anything can go wrong, it will.

There are many variations of this law. Here are some examples:
- If there's a possibility of several things going wrong, the one that will cause the most damage will be the one that goes wrong.
- No matter what goes wrong, it will probably look right.
- Whenever you set out to do something, something else must be done first.
- No matter how long or how hard you shop for an item, after you've bought it it will be on sale somewhere else.
- In order to get a loan, you must first prove you don't need it.

If anything can go wrong, it will. I want to point out to you that this is a man-made law. I do not find Murphy's Law in the Bible, but I know a lot of Christians who believe in it. Who was Murphy, you might ask, and what circumstances inspired him to promulgate this law?

I have found two published versions of the history of Murphy's Law. One dictionary says that the law is probably named after Murphy, a cartoon character who always made mistakes. He appeared in a series of educational cartoons published by the U.S. Navy. I have confirmed that this was so with a Chief Petty Officer who served in the second World War. The U.S. Air Force version of it is that it took place when a

NASA project was in its early stages around 1949. An engineer named Captain Ed Murphy was putting some equipment together and was having trouble with one part. He said about the person who had made this particular part that "If there is any way to do it wrong, he will". Later the U.S. Air Force gave a press conference and an officer said, "Well, one thing we've learned is to try to totally disregard Murphy's Law". Now the whole world seems to know about Murphy's Law.

The question I want to ask is, How can Christians outwit Murphy's Law? How do we go through life and not allow that law to affect us. Remember the law is, If anything can go wrong, it will. You don't want that to happen in your life, and neither do I. So how do we outwit Murphy's Law?

Don't believe it!

The first point I must make is this: Don't believe it! The reason it works in so many people's lives is that they believe it. I've heard people say hundreds of times, "This has gone wrong and that has gone wrong, now I wonder what the third thing is going to be?" They were expecting something to go wrong, for they believed that bad luck always comes in groups of three events. The first step to outwit Murphy's Law is not to believe it, for it is a man-made principle.

Job, in the Old Testament, unfortunately did believe in it. If it is true that Job was one of the earliest books written in the Bible (some scholars think he was the cousin of Abraham and that places him early in the book of Genesis), then man's concept of Murphy's Law has been around a long time. When

Job was wondering why almost everything had gone wrong in his life, he said, "What I feared has come upon me; what I dreaded has happened to me" (Job 3:25 NIV). He was expecting the worst to happen. "What I feared", the one thing he did not want to happen, did. This fear was in his mind. He dwelt upon it, thought about it, wondered what his reaction would be if and when it did happen. He feared it was going to happen—and it happened, because fear is merely faith in reverse. Fear is believing in the negative, faith is believing in the positive. "What I feared has come upon me; what I dreaded has happened to me."

Even though the rest of the world might believe in Murphy's Law, you, as a Christian, do not need to believe in it. That's the best advice I can give you—don't believe it. However, we must acknowledge that things do go wrong in our lives. We must not bury our heads in the sand like an ostrich and say that life is like a bed of roses, because even for Christians life has its tight spots. Let me remind you that when the disciples of Jesus were out in a boat in the middle of the lake with Jesus on board, they still feared for their lives because they thought the boat would go down (see Matthew 8:23-27). So there are times in life even with Jesus on board, even as members of the family of God, when things appear to go wrong. What are we going to do about it? How can we outwit Murphy's Law on those occasions? First, don't believe Murphy's Law.

Take heart!

Now let me share some words of Jesus with you. "I have told you these things, so that in me you may have peace. In this world you will have trouble. But take heart! I have overcome the world" (John 16:33). What is Jesus saying? Whatever happens around me, I still have a deep inward peace. Circumstances can't take that away from me, for peace is always resident within, ready for me to apply whenever I need it. Author Eric Butterworth says that it is not what happens around you and not what happens to you but what happens within you that is important.

I live in the world, and I'm planning to do that for a while longer. Jesus said that in the world I will have trouble. The word "trouble" is translated from a Greek word meaning a constriction. I often think of trouble as one of life's tight spots, such as when you have painted yourself into a corner of the room and now you cannot move. We all go through tight spots in life. They will come, but Jesus said to "take heart" (NIV) or "be of good cheer" (KJV). So there's another principle to learn: when you get into a tight spot, don't react to it. "Be of good cheer"—you don't have to be happy *because* you're in a tight spot, but when you are in a tight spot you can take heart. Don't thank God you have a problem today, but thank God for Christ. Any answer to the tight spots we face is going to be through the Christ Who is within us. He said, "Take heart! I have overcome the world."

You're in training

"Praise be to the God and Father of our Lord Jesus Christ, the Father of compassion and the God of all comfort, who comforts us in all our troubles, so that we can comfort those in any trouble with the comfort we ourselves have received from God" (II Corinthians 1:3–4). God comforts us in all our "troubles"; in our tight spots. So even though we get into them, this verse says that God is around and available and He will comfort you. The word "comfort" suggests He puts His arms around our shoulders and says, "It's going to be okay".

It is God Who comforts us in all our tight spots, and He does it for a good reason: "... so that we can comfort those in any trouble with the comfort we ourselves have received from God." It's a learning experience. We're in training! God wants us to know how to handle tight spots, so that we can help other people to handle their tight spots. The same comfort that God gives to us, we can pass on to other people in the same situation. Perhaps you have heard the American Indian proverb that you "must wear my moccasins before you understand what I'm going through". But once you've been in that situation, then you understand.

Once you've been through bankruptcy in a business, you know how to comfort other people who have failed in business. Once you've had a death in the immediate family, you are able to comfort other people who have had a death in their family. God comforted you when you were there, so you are able to comfort other people. Yes, there are tight spots, things do go wrong, but when they do God comforts us in all our tight spots.

Knocked down but not out

"We are hard pressed on every side, but not crushed; perplexed, but not in despair" (II Corinthians 4:8). The words "hard pressed" come from the same word translated "trouble". There are tight spots on every side, yet since we do not believe in Murphy's Law we do not allow the tight spots to get to us. We see them as just another opportunity to express the Christ within. Paul goes on to say that we are "perplexed", we don't always understand, but we do not despair.

"Persecuted, but not abandoned; struck down, but not destroyed" (verse 9). We might be persecuted, but we know God has not let us down; He has not forsaken us. We might even be struck down but we are not destroyed, or as J.B. Phillips so wonderfully translates it, "we may be knocked down but we are never knocked out!" Since we have Christ within, we can always pick ourselves up and get on with life. So what do we learn from this? Don't react to the circumstances, don't react when they go wrong, don't believe in Murphy's Law. This does not mean that we should take life passively, for there are actions we can do when we are in tight spots.

It's time to rejoice

"Though the fig tree does not bud and there are no grapes on the vines, though the olive crop fails and the fields produce no food, though there are no sheep in the pen and no cattle in the stalls..." (Habakkuk 3:17). Tell you what, that farmer has problems, doesn't he? Agricultural production is down to zero. But what is he going to do about it? "...Yet I will rejoice in the Lord, I will be joyful in God my Saviour. The Sovereign Lord is my strength; he makes my feet like the feet of a deer, he enables me to go on the heights" (Habakkuk 3:18–19a).

What a tremendous statement tucked away in that little book. Even though the fig tree will not bud, yet I will rejoice in the Lord. When things go wrong, when it looks like you, as a Christian, have become a victim of Murphy's Law, one thing you can do is to rejoice in God—not rejoice because life's gone crazy but in that situation rejoice because He is your strength. There is no greater time when you need God's strength than when you're in those situations. When the fig tree doesn't blossom, when the business starts to go down, when nobody places an order this week, then "I will rejoice in the Lord". Recognise that the God and Father of our Lord Jesus Christ has you in His hand, Christ is within and He and you can take care of the situation together.

Perseverance

Paul had been through the same situation himself and he said, "Not only so, but we also rejoice in our sufferings, because we know that suffering produces perseverance" (Romans 5:3). Rejoicing in our sufferings is a strange thing to do. The word for "sufferings" is the same word for "troubles", tight spots. We are to rejoice *in* our tight spots. Paul knew this, because he learnt that tight spots produced perseverance (the Greek word is "endurance"). Tight spots produce endurance or perseverance, and "perseverance, character; and character, hope. And hope does not disappoint us, because God has poured out his love into our hearts by the Holy Spirit, whom he has given us" (Romans 5:4–5).

It was not the first time that Paul had found himself in a tight spot. After a few times he saw them for what they were: life challenging him to believe, opportunities to prove his faith in God. He discovered that tight spots produced endurance, endurance produced experience (character), and experience produced expectation (hope). It's true that what you expect is what you will get. Read the whole passage and really get the depth out of the truth that is there. Paul is saying that when you are in a tight spot, rejoice, because you are about to grow in awareness and that will improve your situation.

When some folk get into a tight spot they throw in the towel. That would be the result of believing in Murphy's Law. However, now you know what is happening you can recognise that you are about to grow in awareness of who you are and what you have, and the end result will be good because of what you have been through. "And we know that in all things God works for the good of those who love him, who have been called according to his purpose " (Romans 8:28). One variation of Murphy's Law is, "Don't believe in miracles, rely on them". That's one of the more positive variations. Perhaps it's the one that suits the Christian viewpoint better than most. "Don't believe in miracles, rely on them." Most miracles are the result of a divine-human reciprocity—God and you working on the situation together.

There's one other verse in Romans I want to share with you. "Be joyful in hope, patient in affliction, faithful in prayer" (Romans 12:12). Patience in affliction, patience in the tight spots. Sitting there and saying, "Okay, I can get through this thing." I've heard many preachers tell about Paul when he had generated a little opposition and had to leave the city in a hurry. The gate had already been locked, so someone let him down in a basket on the end of a rope and he went quickly on his way (see Acts 9:25). When you get to the end of the rope, tie a knot and hang on—that's patience in affliction, that's enduring the tight spots. You do it because God has not left you, He is your strength and you praise Him and rejoice in the Lord.

There is an answer

Yes, there is a Christian answer to Murphy's Law. We can outwit Murphy's Law because we *are* Christians. We don't believe it, we don't react to it, when we do get into trouble we praise God, and we endure the experience because we know we are in training to help others.

Charles Roth, who was the initial inspiration for the first two chapters of this book, said that perhaps we should rephrase Murphy's Law in a positive way. This is what he suggested: "It is humanly and intellectually impossible to constantly guess and provide for every contingency when planning a long-range goal. Therefore, be flexible."

He is saying that it is possible things can go wrong occasionally, so you had better be flexible. The best way to be flexible is to apply the positive principles of God's Word. Jesus said we would have trouble or tight spots, God said He would comfort us during those times, the Bible says to rejoice in Him during those times, and the end result is that we have grown in awareness from the tight spots in life. God's Word teaches us to throw out Murphy's Law and to replace it with God's positive principles.

Chapter Three
How to Outperform the Peter Principle

*J*ust in case you think I'm the one who invented the principle, I have to disclaim ownership, and gladly so. The Peter Principle was proclaimed by Dr Lawrence Peter, who said that in a hierarchy every employee tends to rise to his or her level of incompetence. If the principle is true, then there is plenty of incompetence around—in organisations, in businesses, yes, even in churches.

Dr Peter had observed in business particularly (he was a consultant to business as well as a scholar and academic) that there were many people who did a fine job at one stage of their career but when they were elevated to a higher position they were not able to cope. In fact, they became obviously incompetent at that higher level. His book titled *The Peter Principle* was published in 1969 and it has since sold over 6 million copies, which is an excellent response for any book. It is now such a well-accepted principle that it is listed in the dictionary: The Peter Principle, the theory that in a hierarchy every employee tends to rise to a level just beyond his level of competence.

In another publication, *The Book of Lists*, Dr Peter has listed some of the famous historical people whom he believes had risen to their level of incompetence. He says Socrates was a competent teacher who reached the level of incompetence when he became his own defence attorney. If you recall he lost his own case and finished up having to drink poison. Julius Caesar, he said, also put the principle into action. He was one of the great generals of all times, but he became too trusting in his relations with politicians. We should all learn a lesson from that, because eventually they killed him. Nero, he says, was a competent fiddler who achieved his level of incompetence as an administrator. Adolf Hitler, the consummate politician, found his level of incompetence as a generalissimo.

That is the principle, and there are a lot of people in the business world who know exactly what you are talking about when you mention the Peter Principle. Many of them believe in it and they can probably give you examples of it in operation. Now I'm not denying that there are valid examples, for in the companies for which I have worked there were some classic examples that I might be tempted to label as fine illustrations of the Peter Principle. But what I'm concerned with is this: How does it apply to Christians, who have faith in God, a God who leads and guides them? How can we outperform the Peter Principle, and do we have a level of incompetence?

Don't believe it!

The number one way to outperform the Peter Principle is: Don't believe it. Can you find a reference anywhere in God's Word where it says that you will become incompetent? Not in my copy of the Bible. It's a man-made principle. I think it was clever advertising to call it the Peter "Principle" in the first place. A principle is something that works every time it is applied. Put together two parts of hydrogen and one part of oxygen, and what do you get? Water—it's a principle, a fixed law.

The Peter Principle does *not* work every time, for you can go into many businesses and organisations and find examples of people who have risen until they have reached the top position in the company but remain intensely competent. So the first thing is not to believe it, because there are many examples to show that the "principle" does not always work, therefore it is not a principle.

The second thing I want to say is that when the opportunity comes for you to rise to another level, whether it be in your regular employment, a part-time business you are operating or whatever, you can tap into God's guidance. Guidance is always available. Perhaps God's plan for your life does not include you being the Chief Executive Officer of the largest company in your field. Maybe God knows you have a better opportunity to fulfil your life's dream in middle management or somewhere else in the corporate ladder, or perhaps even as a self-employed person.

Let me share with you this beautiful verse, "Whether you turn to the right or to the left, your ears will hear a voice behind you, saying, 'This is the way; walk in it'" (Isaiah 30:21 NIV). God is saying that He will guide you at all times if you will listen. Just because somebody comes up to you and offers you a position at a higher level in the organisational structure, it does not mean you have to accept it. What you should do is to listen for God's guidance. Not every job is going to suit you and you are not going to suit every job. I know a man who was out of work when someone offered him a job for a considerable amount of money but his guidance was not to take that job. When the company had difficulties later, he understood why.

The second way to outperform the Peter Principle is to recognise that God can guide you in your life's career, as well as in everything else. You don't have to rise to a level of incompetence, you can seek God's guidance and say, "Okay, Father, do you really want me to have this job? Am I going to really fulfil my life's purpose doing that, or should I stay where I am for a little while if you have something better around the next corner?" God's guidance is available and if we learn to walk by it, I believe we would always be at the level of our competence because we would be doing what God wants us to do. So listen to that "voice behind you". Sometimes it might say to go a different road, for God has planned something far better for you.

How do you learn to walk by God's guidance? Well, I've always encouraged people to listen when looking for a parking spot. "Where is it, Lord? Should I turn left into Hindmarsh Square, or should I go further down Pulteney Street or should I go over to Frome Street?" God's guidance is available in all of life's situations. If you learn to operate it at the parking-spot level, then when somebody comes up to you and says, "I've got just the job for you. It's going to pay $100,000 per year", before you sell your soul to that kind of situation, listen to the voice of God and you will find it will be more than helpful.

Accept God's competence

The best way for a Christian to outperform the Peter Principle is to accept God's competence for your life. There is a great example in the book of Exodus that I want to share with you. "Then Moses said to the Israelites, 'See, the Lord has chosen Bezalel son of Uri, the son of Hur, of the tribe of Judah, and he has filled him with the Spirit of God, with skill, ability and knowledge in all kinds of crafts...'" (Exodus 35:30-31). That is incredible! God has placed within this person skill, ability, and knowledge. To do what? "... 'To make artistic designs for work in gold, silver and bronze, to cut and set stones, to work in wood and to engage in all kinds of artistic craftsmanship. And he has given both him and Oholiab son of Ahisamach, of the tribe of Dan, the ability to teach others. He has filled them with skill to do all kinds of work as craftsmen, designers, embroiderers in blue, purple and scarlet yarn and fine linen, and weavers—all of them master craftsmen and designers'" (Exodus 35:32-35).

Way back in Old Testament days when the nation of Israel was wandering around in the wilderness, God gave to these men workmanship abilities. As you read on in this passage you will see that the intricate items that they wrought with their hands were of the highest level of workmanship in those fields—gold and silver and jewellery and clothing. It was top quality stuff. The top fashion designer would have been thrilled to put his name on the clothing that was produced, yet it was God Who gave Bezalel and Oholiab the ability to do it. God put His spirit of competence upon them.

God still does that, and that thought opens up a whole world of new possibilities. If I'm involved in a particular situation and I need help to do the top-quality job that my professionalism demands, then I have God's help in that situation. He gives me the wisdom I need, He gives me the knowledge, He gives me the ability. Rich, divine, prospering ideas will flow to me if I recognise this possibility. So I'm just going to laugh at the Peter Principle, all the way to the bank, because with that ability there will be no shortage of people wanting my services.

Let's now ask, "Are Christians competent people?" "Not that we are competent in ourselves to claim anything for ourselves, but our competence comes from God" (II Corinthians 3:5). Since my competence comes from God, then it is impossible for me to rise to a level of incompetence. It has now become a contradiction of terms.

The thought is amplified in verse 6, which says that God "... has made us competent as ministers of a new covenant—not of the letter but of the Spirit; for the letter kills, but the Spirit gives life" (II Corinthians 3:6). Isn't that a tremendous passage? So my competence, my ability, my sufficiency is from God. That is why the Peter Principle does not apply to a Christian, because every Christian is tapped into

God, the great fountain-head of knowledge and wisdom and workmanship.

Recognise God's nature within

One final way to outperform the Peter Principle is to recognise that God's nature is resident within you. "Through these he has given us his very great and precious promises, so that through them you may participate in [partake of, KJV) the divine nature and escape the corruption in the world caused by evil desires" (II Peter 1:4).

Now since it is true that I have partaken of God's nature, I must simply ask the question, "Is God competent?" Of course God is competent. The whole material creation proves His competence. Therefore I have within me that competent nature. I can no longer go around saying "I'm only human". I am a unique combination of the human and the divine. So if there is anything I need to know in my job, I need only to tap into His wisdom, His competence.

If God could give two Jewish men wandering around the wilderness the ability to make the best jewellery and the best clothes in the world, what can He do for His own sons and daughters in this age of modern technology? Do you know there are many things God has placed in this universe that He is still waiting for some of His sons and daughters to discover? You go out into your garden and you say, "I'll have to do something about those weeds". Why do we call that plant a weed? Only because humanity has yet to find a use for it. The lowly peanut or groundnut was a weed until George Washington Carver, the great black agricultural chemist, discovered its food value and oil content. He derived more than 300 products from the lowly peanut. The world is waiting for you to discover hidden treasures in nature, better ways for mankind to accomplish worthwhile things.

How do you outperform the Peter Principle? Don't believe it, for since you are a Christian it does not apply to you; you are tapped into something far better. Then recognise that God's guidance is available in all situations. Thirdly, accept God's competence, and lastly, remember you are a container of the divine nature and because of this you have outperformed the Peter Principle.

Chapter Four

How to Have God as Your Partner

Recently I read an article which told the story of how an accountant started a business as a garbage collector and after two years had a gross income of $2 million and within 10 years had a business in all the large cities of America. Apparently in his area the garbage collection was handled by a community committee. He went along to the committee meeting one night and was told that the company who had the contract for garbage collection would be quitting on Friday night and there was nobody to take it over. Being an accountant and also a young man who felt that almost anything could be done, the next morning he called the chairman and said, "I'll take care of the garbage collection."

So he got knee deep in garbage from around 3 o'clock to 8 o'clock every morning, and then went on to his accounting practice for the rest of the day. Of course, he put in many long hours and long months, but eventually he made it profitable. Then he took on his financial adviser as a partner, and they set up companies in every major U.S. city.

There are many people in business who get to the stage where they need to take on a partner. Either they need somebody else's expertise, or somebody's information in a particular area to help their company fulfil its goals, or they need some extra capital. Of course, when a business takes on a partner, the partner wants some share of the profits. It may be an equal partnership where profits are split evenly, it might be a capital venture situation where the partner puts in the money but has no day-by-day involvement in how the business is run, or it may be a controlling partner who tells the management how to run the business.

Let's apply this to your life, the company known as You and Yourself Incorporated. We all need partners to help us through life. However, when you have a partner, there are responsibilities, so first you should sign an agreement. Nothing will ruin a partnership quicker than just shaking hands on it. You need an agreement stating the responsibilities of each partner. Having done that, you need to talk to your partner on a regular basis, especially over the decision-making process. As the Bible says, "For lack of guidance a nation falls, but many advisers make victory sure" (Proverbs 11:14 NIV).

Now I believe that God wants to be a partner in your life. I'm not just talking about becoming a member of God's forever family, that is, a Christian. I'm talking about inviting God into every area of your life and saying, "Okay, God, it's you and me. We'll work this together and make a success of it". I want to share with you three Bible examples of people who took God as their partner and, as a result of doing so they were successful in life.

Jacob's partnership with God
Let's look at a small part of the life of Jacob, that wonderful man whose name became part of the description of God—the God of Abraham, Isaac and Jacob. He obviously had a high standing in the nation of Israel. One night Jacob "...had a dream in which he saw a stairway resting on the earth, with its top reaching to heaven, and the angels of God were ascending and descending on it. There above it stood the Lord, and he said: 'I am the Lord, the God of your father Abraham and the God of Isaac. I will give you and your descendants the land on which you are lying. Your descendants will be like the dust of the earth, and you will spread out to the west and to the east, to the north and to the south. All peoples on earth will be blessed through you and your offspring. I am with you and will watch over you wherever you go, and I will bring you back to this land. I will not leave you until I have done what I have promised you.'

"When Jacob awoke from his sleep, he thought, 'Surely the Lord is in this place, and I was not aware of it.' He was afraid and said, 'How awesome is this place! This is none other than the house of God; this is the gate of heaven.' Early the next morning Jacob took the stone he had placed under his head and set it up as a pillar and poured oil on top of it. He called that place Bethel, though the city used to be called Luz. Then Jacob made a vow, saying, 'If God will be with me and will watch over me on this journey I am taking and will give me food to eat and clothes to wear so that I return safely to my father's house, then the Lord will be my God and this stone that I have set up as a pillar will be God's house, and of all that you give me I will give you a tenth'" (Gen. 28:12-22).

This is the partnership agreement: God agreed to be with Jacob, to feed and clothe him, and provide him with a large family. Jacob agreed to the deal, and then to seal it he agreed to recompense God for the expertise and capital that he was putting in by giving to God 10% of the receipts, the turnover, of the company. Not 10% of the profits, but 10% of the receipts. That's quite an agreement, isn't it?

God wants a similar agreement with you and me. God wants us to take Him as a partner, and in the partnership agreement God says He will take care of the food, the clothing, the shelter, the peace, the happiness, the joy that we need. He will take care of the decision-making in the partnership, the guidance that we need, the path to take in various situations, and for all that He wants recompense. Not the 10% off the top as in the Old Testament, but in the New Testament era He asks us to name the percentage. "For with the measure you use, it will be measured to you" (Luke 6:38b). God, as your partner, requires a return on His investment and the commitment you and I have to make is that we will follow His guidance and see that He gets His portion. As Oral Roberts has well said, "you cannot outgive God". You name the percentage and see how much God blesses you.

So Jacob had a beautiful partnership agreement. Note that in verse 20 it says, "Jacob made a vow". That was his agreement. That was the legal document upon which he was going to operate the rest of his life. You only have to read on through Genesis to find out how well he did. He finished up having 12 sons, and in order to feed and keep 12 sons you need a very good income. Today they would cost you a fortune before you got them married off!

Israel's partnership with God

I want to show you now that God went beyond dealing with an individual like Jacob. He made a partnership agreement with the whole nation of Israel, and in Deuteronomy chapter 26 this agreement is summarised. "The Lord your God commands you this day to follow these decrees and laws; carefully observe them with all your heart and with all your soul. You have declared this day that the Lord is your God and that you will walk in his ways, that you will keep his decrees, commands and laws, and that you will obey him. And the Lord has declared this day that you are his people, his treasured possession as he promised, and that you are to keep all his commands. He has declared that he will set you in praise, fame and honour high above all the nations he has made and that you will be a people holy to the Lord your God, as he promised" (Deuteronomy 26:16–19).

The nation of Israel agreed to follow God and God agreed to make them the best nation upon earth. What was God's recompense for all this? They too were to give 10% off the top to various causes close to the heart of God. "When you have finished setting aside a tenth of all your produce in the third year, the year of the tithe, you shall give it to the Levite, the alien, the fatherless and the widow, so that they may eat in your towns and be satisfied" (Deuteronomy 26:12).

When you read the Old Testament you see that whenever the people of Israel kept their part of the agreement, they prospered. They prospered even more greatly than the nation of Egypt, which was probably the richest country on earth prior to this time. Israel was one of the greatest trading nations of the world. While it was partly because of their geographical location, the real reason was because of God's blessing. Whenever they followed the way that God laid down, they were blessed. When they didn't follow it, they got into trouble. In fact, you might remember that they finally turned their backs on God and were carried off into Babylon and they spent decades there in slavery. Yes, the agreement works, but it's a partnership and each partner has to pull his weight in the partnership. As long as Israel pulled its weight, then God's blessing was there.

Peter and his partners

Now let's look at a New Testament example of a partnership, found in Luke chapter 5. Jesus had a need, and that was for a boat from which he could preach and teach the Word of God to the multitudes of people. There was an enormous crowd and he wanted to get out a little, so that everybody could hear. There happened to be two ships standing by the lake, and Jesus went to Simon Peter and asked him if he could use his fishing boat. When he was invited on board, he sat down and taught the people.

So the need of Jesus was met because Simon allowed him the use of his boat. Now Jesus is ready to do His part in the partnership.

"When he had finished speaking, he said to Simon, 'Put out into deep water, and let down the nets for a catch.' Simon answered, 'Master, we've worked hard all night and haven't caught anything...'" (Luke 5:4–5a). Peter and his two companions are called partners in verses 7 and 10. James, John and Peter had a three-way partnership in a fishing business. They were expert fisherman. This was their livelihood; they had done this day in and day out for years. They knew the Sea of Galilee, they knew all its many moods, they knew how to tell when to go fishing and when not to, and where to go and so on. But on this particular night all their expertise had failed them.

"'Master, we've worked hard all night and haven't caught anything. But because you say so, I will let down the nets.' When they had done so, they caught such a large number of fish that their nets began to break. So they signalled their partners in the other boat to come and help them, and they came and filled both boats so full that they began to sink" (Luke 5:5b–7). That was quite a fishing trip when you think about it. Simon Peter already had partners, but what he needed was some extra expertise. Peter had obviously heard that Jesus was teaching people that God was a good God, that God wanted to meet their needs, that every individual had a right to approach God and receive His blessing. Peter must have recognised Jesus as a teacher, for he used the word "Master".

"But because you say so, I will let down the nets", and when he did he got the result that God had planned for him. When you take an action based on the Word of God, you get good results—a net-breaking, ship-sinking, abundant result! I suggest to you that in your life you have or will have opportunities where you need extra expertise, you need extra information that is not available from any other source, and God has it for you. There are times in life when you need extra capital, extra power to enable you to accomplish what you want to do. Often you find that it is not available from human sources, and then you can thank God you and He are partners, that you are on His team, a winning team.

Watch your partnerships

One of the great dangers of partnerships on a human level is that you can get involved with the wrong people. There is nothing that can drag you down more quickly than setting up a partnership with the wrong person. "Do not be yoked together with unbelievers. For what do righteousness and wickedness have in common? Or what fellowship can light have with darkness? What harmony is there between Christ and Belial? What does a believer have in common with an unbeliever? What agreement is there between the temple of God and idols? For we are the temple of the living God. As God has said: 'I will live with them and walk among them, and I will be their God, and they will be my people'" (II Corinthians 6:14–16). With the rich, divine, prospering ideas that come out of a partnership with God, who would want to have a partnership with the wrong people? However, the warning is clear and God's Word is saying to Christians to be careful with whom you get involved.

Our best partnership

"We have come to share in Christ if we hold firmly till the end the confidence we had at first" (Hebrews 3:14). The words "to share" come from the same Greek word family used in Luke where it spoke about Peter's partners. Some translations do use the word "partner", such as Rotherham: "For partners of the Christ have we become." That's a beautiful concept: Christ and I are in business together. I have Christ within, so I'm tapped into all of His wisdom, all His guidance, all His power, all His peace, all His ability to relate to people, all His ability to cut through the chaff and get to the basic issues that need to be handled. I have a partner Who has all the expertise I will ever need and has all the capital I'm ever going to need. It's a thrilling partnership to be "partners of the Christ". It goes beyond just being in the family of God. It is making a total commitment, a quality commitment, to make the partnership work.

God and I are partners and He will take care of certain aspects of our business and as a part of His recompense for doing so, I'm going to share a percentage of the receipts of the business with him. Together we will make a success out of my life. Do you believe that? I certainly do and I know you can when you have God as your partner. He's an expert at the impossible and the unbelievable. Make a quality commitment today to work your partnership with God and then enjoy the benefits that will flow from it.

Chapter Five

How to Win With God's Weapons

*I*t so often seems that in the Bible, as well as in everyday life, the things God uses to take care of situations that we need fixed are often unusual, out of the ordinary. You and I would not normally choose these ways in which to solve a problem, but our God does and He's a great big wonderful God.

If I had been Samson, I might not have chosen to pick up the jaw of an ass and win that victory. If I had been David, I wouldn't have picked up five little stones from a brook to kill a great giant. If I had been Moses, I wouldn't have held up my rod to part the Red Sea—I would have thought about constructing barges to get the people across. If I had been Joshua, I certainly wouldn't have marched around the walls of Jericho, once a day for six days and seven times on the last day, and expected the city to give in to me. If it had been me, I would have missed that glorious victory. God uses unusual and different things in life in order to bring glory to Himself and to make the victory a memorable one. "For the foolishness of God is wiser than man's wisdom, and the weakness of God is stronger than man's strength" (I Corinthians 1:25 NIV).

In the book of Judges, chapter 7, we have the record of Gideon, a man that we hear very little of prior to this incident. In the previous chapter God sent an angel to this man one day to inform him that he had been chosen to deliver the nation of Israel. At the time they were under siege by the Midian army, who were causing incredible problems.

Gideon wasn't sure about this commission. He told the angel that he was not a great man, not good with words, not a general of the army, and eventually he ran out of excuses. But the angel said, "You're the one. God is going to use you, so just do what He tells you to do and there will be victory." Gideon gathered together an army of 32,000 to face an enemy numbering 15,000 men—that's better than a 2 to 1 advantage. Then God sent him another message.

The tests

"The Lord said to Gideon, 'You have too many men for me to deliver Midian into their hands. In order that Israel may not boast against me that her own strength has saved her, announce now to the people, "Anyone who trembles with fear may turn back and leave Mount Gilead".' So twenty-two thousand men left, while ten thousand remained" (Judges 7:2–3).

Prior to this the nation had turned their back on God, and God wants it to be certain that the credit for the victory will be His. That the bulk of the army did not have a strong faith in God is clear, for 22,000 men who "trembled with fear" went home. To co-operate in a victory with God, you must totally believe in Him.

Gideon is now down to an army of 10,000 and that's 2 to 3 against. Now I would have thought that ratio would have proved the point, but God thought otherwise. 10,000 with God on your side is a waste of resources, so another test was called for.

"But the Lord said to Gideon, 'There are still too many men. Take them down to the water, and I will sift them for you there...' There the Lord told him, 'Separate those who lap the water with their tongues like a dog from those who kneel down to drink.' Three hundred men lapped with their hands to their mouths. All the rest got down on their knees to drink. The Lord said to Gideon, 'With the three hundred men that lapped I will save you and give the Midianites into your hands. Let all the other men go, each to his own place.' So Gideon sent the rest of the Israelites to their tents but kept the three hundred, who took over the provisions and trumpets of the others. Now the camp of Midian lay below him in the valley" (Judges 7:4–8).

I think the test was devised because when a man gets on his knees to drink the water straight out of the stream, he is vulnerable to attack. The one that gets the water up in his hands is looking around and is aware of his circumstances. Only 300 men passed the test. Now how's that for odds, 300 against 15,000, 1 against 50? The victory could have been achieved with less, but God said that was enough.

The plan

Let's look at the strategic plan that God used. "During that night the Lord said to Gideon, 'Get up, go down against the camp, because I am going to give it into your hands. If you are afraid to attack, go down to the camp with your servant Purah and listen to what they are saying. Afterward, you will be encouraged to attack the camp.' So he and Purah his servant went down to the outposts of the camp. The Midianites, the Amalekites and all the other eastern peoples had settled in the valley, thick as locusts. Their camels could no more be counted than the sand on the seashore. Gideon arrived just as a man was telling a friend his dream. 'I had a dream,' he was saying. 'A round loaf of barley bread came tumbling into the Midianite camp. It struck the tent with such force that the tent overturned and collapsed.'" (Judges 7:9-13).

How understanding God is, because He knew that Gideon was fearful of the situation. This man, who had never been a general, had seen his army reduced from 32,000 men to 300. I think I would have asked the Lord for reinforcements! The Lord told Gideon to spy on the enemy and see what they were talking about. Gideon and his servant heard the soldier tell of his dream, and then they were astonished when the soldier's friend interpreted the dream. "His friend responded, 'This can be nothing other than the sword of Gideon son of Joash, the Israelite. God has given the Midianites and the whole camp into his hands.' When Gideon heard the dream and its interpretation, he worshipped God. He returned to the camp of Israel and called out, 'Get up! The Lord has given the Midianite camp into your hands'" (Judges 7:14-15).

When Gideon heard the telling of the dream and its interpretation, he probably just said under his breath, "Well, praise God!" He returned to his army and boldly declared that God has given the Midianites and the whole camp into their hands. That was a powerful statement of faith. I'm sure God inspired that dream and God inspired the interpretation of it. It just so happened that it took place in the tent outside of which Gideon and his servant were listening. God works in mysterious ways, His wonders to perform!

The weapons

Let's look at the weapons they used. Gideon divided the 300 men into three companies. He put a trumpet in each man's hand and an empty pitcher or jar with a lamp inside. What strange weapons! "'Watch me,' he told them. 'Follow my lead. When I get to the edge of the camp, do exactly as I do. When I and all who are with me blow our trumpets, then from all around the camp blow yours and shout, "For the Lord and for Gideon".'" (Judges 7:17–18).

I'd loved to have heard those trumpets, wouldn't you? You've probably heard that song about 76 trombones. I wonder what 301 trumpets would have sounded like. 300 men plus Gideon makes 301 trumpets blasting out in the middle of the night. What a great show! I wish I had been there. Over 15,000 people were, but I'm sure that all of them did not enjoy it.

The weapons that God used are symbolic of the weapons that God has given to help us fight our battles. First of all, each man was given a trumpet. Now the trumpet in the Bible is often used as a symbol for the voice of God. For example, in the book of Revelation, John says, "On the Lord's Day I was in the Spirit, and I heard behind me a loud voice like a trumpet" (Revelation 1:10). He is speaking of the voice of God. You have that same privilege of having the voice of God to guide you in the conquests in which you are involved. "Whether you turn to the right or to the left, your ears will hear a voice behind you, saying, 'This is the way; walk in it'" (Isaiah 30:21). God wants to guide His people, but do you know what the problem is? The problem is not with God, it's with us—our deaf ears. We so often tune out the commercials on radio and television, tune out the wife or the husband when they talk, that we also tune out the voice of God. We should stop and get quiet and say, "Father, which way is it?" The voice of God is available to you and to me. If we will but listen and apply God's direction, we will win the battle. So the trumpet has significance—it is the voice of God guiding and directing us in the battle.

Every man also had a lamp in his hand. "Your word is a lamp to my feet and a light for my path" (Psalm 119:105). We have God's Word, we know what is God's plan for our lives, we know that God wants for us only health, wealth and happiness. We also know that between us and that goal there are always "Midianites", the challenges and opportunities that we have to handle before we can enjoy the blessing. We need to rely on God's Word to guide us. So there are the weapons—the trumpet—the voice of God, and the lamp—the Word of God.

However, notice that the lamp was inside a clay jar. Clay in the Bible talks about humanity. We are but clay, we are made from the dust, we are just "mud babies", as my friend Steve Heefner says. So what does the jar signify? We'll see that graphically in the next few verses. "Gideon and the hundred men with him reached the edge of the camp at the beginning of the middle watch, just after they had changed the guard. They blew their trumpets and broke the jars that were in their hands. The three companies blew the trumpets and smashed the jars. Grasping the torches in their left hands and holding in their right hands the trumpets they were to blow, they shouted, 'A sword for the Lord and for Gideon!' While each man held his position around the camp, all the Midianites ran, crying out as they fled. When the three hundred trumpets sounded, the Lord caused the men throughout the camp to turn on each other with their swords. The army fled to Beth Shittah toward Zererah as far as the border of Abel Meholah near Tabbath" (Judges 7:19–22b).

What happened to the jars? They were broken so that the light could shine forth. Emerson put it well when he said that we should "release the imprisoned splendour". We are to show to the world the Christ within. Many of us are yet to allow the splendour to shine forth. We have yet to get our mind aligned with God's strategy of victory. I'm not teaching the concept of self-denial and brokenness, nor the religious concept of doing things to show humility, the ashes-and-sackcloth routine, but I am saying that we must not allow our humanity to get in the way of God's program for our lives. We excuse it and we rationalise it by saying, "Well, I'm only human, of course." But that is an error. You are not only human; you have divinity within you, you have Christ in you the hope of glory. You are human and divine, and it's the human part of you that stops the divine part showing. That's why they broke the jars and let the light shine forth upon the enemy.

I would love to have been there! I would like to see the record produced as a television mini-series. In the middle of the night, when they were comfortable in their tents, not expecting any action, all of a sudden 301 trumpets blasted out, enough to wake up the dead, and then the crack of broken crockery falling to the ground, and when they poked their heads out of the tent flap they saw a ring of light right around the camp. I think I would have done exactly the same as the Midianites did. I would have got up out of bed and still in my pyjamas I would have run. And that's what they did. They became so confused they started killing each other, for they didn't know who was the enemy and who wasn't. And the army fled through various towns right to the Jordan River.

What can we learn from this great record? How do we win using God's weapons? We use the trumpet, listening for the voice of God. We use the lamp, the Word of God, steadfast and sure. We have Christ within, permanently and with potential, and we release the imprisoned splendour. 50 to 1 against were the odds, but with God on their side they won. With God's weapons you can always win but it takes people of faith, people totally convinced what God has said about them to co-operate with God and get the victory. God wants men and women who will do one thing and that is believe—believe His Word, believe what He says to do even when it may look foolish. Yes, you can win life's battles using God's weapons.

Chapter Six

How to Have a Successful Year

*E*verybody wants to have a successful year. We want a year in which we can enjoy all the blessings of God. I have a simple secret to share with you, as well as a concept from a beautiful passage in the book of Proverbs. How can you have a successful year? Well, you put together a string of successful months. How can you have a successful month? You put together a string of successful weeks. How can you have a successful week? You put together a string of successful days. Are you getting the message? How can you have a successful day? You put together a string of successful hours. Now it's in an area where it is easier to handle.

The task may look enormous and daunting when

you think of the coming year—whether it's a calendar year or a financial year or just a year from now. So much is possible in the space of one year and so much effort might be necessary to bring your personal plans and purposes to fruition. However, if you realise that the only time you can control is not the rest of this year but right now, then you should be concerned with how to make this hour a successful hour. So take the year an hour at a time, a day at a time, a week at a time. Jesus said as much in the Sermon on the Mount, "Therefore do not worry about tomorrow, for tomorrow will worry about itself. Each day has enough trouble of its own" (Matthew 6:34 NIV). We could rephrase it in a positive form and say, "Each day has the right amount of good". God wants us to live one day at a time, and if we do that, then it's going to be a tremendous year.

In the book of Proverbs, chapter 3, there are some principles that we can apply to make this year a successful year.

Keep God's principles

"My son, do not forget my teaching, but keep my commands in your heart" (Proverbs 3:1). Verses 1 to 4 of this chapter are introductory and then verses 5 to 10 give us some definite principles. The "heart" in this whole passage does not refer to some inner part of your being—it's the seat of your personal life, the mind. For example, "For as he thinketh in his heart, so is he" (Proverbs 23:7 KJV). The mind is where the thinking process takes place.

I love the way the Jerusalem Bible renders Proverbs 3:1, "My son, do not forget my teaching, let your heart keep my principles." I believe that God is a God of principle. God has laid down successful principles for all who believe in Him. God does not have a string of separate concepts to suit your life and another string to suit my life. One thing I do not believe in is what is called the "capricious will of God", that is, He is going to bless Joe today and the rest of us can get through as best we can. If that's the kind of God we have, then we will never know when it is our day. We will probably start looking at the stars or get our biorhythm calculators out and try to figure if today is going to be our good day. That is what is meant by a capricious will and it is not what the Bible teaches. Certainly God is sovereign, but since He stands behind His Word He limits Himself by it, and therefore abides by His own principles. "I the Lord do not change..." (Malachi 3:6). God's will for you and for me is unchanging. We can thank God for that, because it means that God has laid down principles, and if we understand those principles then every day can be a beautiful day. God wants us to keep His principles in our minds. If we do, then when the need arises we can apply them.

The introduction continues, "For they [God's principles] will prolong your life many years and bring you prosperity. Let love and faithfulness never leave you; bind them around your neck, write them on the tablet of your heart [mind]" (Proverbs 3:2–3). As you apply the principles, you are promised a long life and prosperity, so spend some time drilling them into your mind. Computers never make a mistake, so they tell us. So who makes the mistakes? The people who write the programs or type in the information. Garbage in, garbage out. Often you have to go back to the manual, find out where you have gone wrong and then apply the principle. So spend time drilling God's principles into your mind.

"Then you will win favour and a good name in the sight of God and man" (Proverbs 3:4), or as the KJV margin says, "... and good success". As a Christian you have favour in the sight of God. Applying His principles produces good success.

The principle of trust

Here's the first principle: "Trust in the Lord with all your heart [mind] and lean not on your own understanding" (Proverbs 3:5). It's the mind that trusts in the Lord. To trust means to rely on, to have confidence in a person or object. Have confidence in God with all your mind in the year that lies ahead. James 1:8 tells us that there are some people who are "double-minded", who are "unstable" in all they do. One moment they think they should go this way and the next moment that way, and soon they are unstable, unsure, undecided what to do. God does not want us to be double-minded but to have a single purpose of trusting in the Lord.

This is a principle that you and I can apply daily. It will not cost you anything except some application, some effort. To emphasise the totality of the trust required in the Lord, the verse continues, "And lean not on your own understanding". Many times we think we know best, but it is not so. God knows best—it's specific and exclusive. God asks us to trust Him totally and completely.

The principle of acknowledgment

Verse 6 brings us the second principle. "In all your ways acknowledge him, and he will make your paths straight" (Proverbs 3:6). How do you acknowledge Him? You recognise that He is with you. Hebrews 11:6 says, "Anyone who comes to him must believe that he exists and that he rewards those who earnestly seek him." Believe these two things: He exists and He rewards with the best those who put their trust in Him. Acknowledge His presence in every part of your life—in your family, in your business, in your personal life. When you do, He will "make your paths straight". He will guide you. The Jerusalem Bible renders it, "He will see that your paths are smooth". Moffat says that "He will clear the road for you". For those who believe that He exists and that He rewards those who seek Him, it's straight ahead down a clear road.

The first Greek translation of the Old Testament is called the Septuagint, because it was prepared by seventy people. They translate this verse in the same way as the King James version does in II Timothy 2:15, "rightly dividing" your paths. The picture is of us coming to a fork in the road. God will guide us as to which road to take. He will direct your path, He will guide you in the way you need to go. I need God's guidance this year, and I am sure you do too. If I had to believe all the guidance I've read in the newspaper over the last week as to what is going to happen in the next twelve months, I could go crazy. In fact, I would probably say, "Stop the world! I want to get off". Thankfully, as I acknowledge Him, He will direct my paths.

The principle of reverence

The next two verses give us our third principle. "Do not be wise in your own eyes; fear the Lord and shun evil. This will bring health to your body and nourishment to your bones" (Proverbs 3:7–8). To fear the Lord means to have a reverence for Him, the God Who made the heavens and the earth, the God Who sent His Son to die on the cross for you and for me. Have a reverence for God and shun evil. Perhaps by now you have noticed that nearly all of these principles have a positive and a negative side to them. "Trust in the Lord with all your heart (the positive), and lean not on your own understanding (the negative)", and here again, "Do not be wise in your own eyes (the negative); fear the Lord (the positive) and shun evil (the negative again)." Turn your back on those things which are not going to be effective in your life this year. Make what some people call a quality decision not to do certain things, because they do not contribute to your success.

The result of applying the principle is clearly stated, "This will bring health to your body and nourishment to your bones". The word "health" is also translated "medicine". God's health care plan is a spiritual medicine that you can administer every time you put God in the right place in your life.

The principle of giving

One further principle is given in verses 9 and 10, and this one hits the wallet or the purse. "Honour the Lord with your wealth, with the firstfruits of all your crops; then your barns will be filled to overflowing, and your vats will brim over with new wine" (Proverbs 3:9–10). They were to honour God with their money and the first portion of the crops, "off the top". God is not saying He wanted their capital, so relax, sit back and enjoy the rest of the chapter! What

God is saying is that he wanted the first portion of their income. The income that has been produced by employing their capital and sufficiency. In Old Testament times the believers had been trained to give the first 10% straight off the top, no questions asked. Every now and then there were special offerings that they were required to make. Someone has calculated that the Jewish people were giving close to 25% of all their income to God. The firstfruits, the first part, was God's system of taxation, because it was a requirement. In fact, God said that if they did not give it then He would charge them interest. It would have been cheaper to borrow from the bank than to take God's rightful firstfruits.

We are not under that system but we are to apply the same proportional principle: "Give, and it will be given to you" (Luke 6:38). We are to give out of our income. We, too, honour God by our giving. It's not enough to go through this year and say, "Yes I trust in God, I acknowledge Him, I reverence Him, but I don't want to give". If you do this, you will have a pretty miserable year and will have to work it out for yourself when things don't go right. However, honour Him with the firstfruit of your crops and "then your barns will be filled to overflowing, and your vats will brim over with new wine". That certainly sounds like prosperity to me!

New wine is a figure of prosperity and affluence in the Bible. So God's promise is available to you and God's principle is for you to take the first step and give Him a percentage of your income. Give it in faith out of what you have. You may not know how you are going to get by with the balance but you will, because it's a principle. Now it is on God's shoulders to fulfil His part of the principle and guide you in a way that will fill your barns with plenty. A similar statement is given in Malachi, chapter 3. "'Bring the whole tithe into the storehouse, that there may be food in my house. Test me in this,' says the Lord Almighty, 'and see if I will not throw open the floodgates of heaven and pour out so much blessing that you will not have room enough for it.'" (Malachi 3:10).

God says to test Him out, and you do it by giving. Take your hands off your gift and thank the Father for giving you those rich, divine, prospering ideas that are going to fill your barns to overflowing. It's a great principle and I'm glad so many Christians believe it and apply it because it helps keep their lives going, it helps fulfil their desires. It is, in fact, an investment in their future.

In conclusion

So God has four principles for us to apply in order to have a successful year. They are simple principles that anyone can apply. If you are marking your Bible, underline these words: verse 5, "trust"; verse 6, "acknowledge"; verse 7, "fear"; and verse 9, "honour". "Do not forget my teaching, let your heart [mind] keep my principles" (Proverbs 3:1 Jerusalem Bible). And remember, to have a successful year you start by making today a successful day, making this week a successful week.

Chapter Seven

How to Keep Your Head Out of a Lion's Mouth

*B*e self-controlled and alert. Your enemy the devil prowls around like a roaring lion looking for someone to devour. Resist him, standing firm in the faith..." (I Peter 5:8–9a NIV). You are a victorious son or daughter of God. That is an unchanging truth. However, it is also true that you have an enemy—a defeated enemy and that only makes him madder. That enemy is out to get you. He is like a boxer in the ring who has lost the fight, the bell has gone yet he wants to keep on fighting. He's defeated, but he won't quit. The fact that you have an enemy should not fill you with fear but it should encourage you to re-examine the strength that God has given to you so that you can handle your enemy, the devil.

"Your adversary…" (KJV) is the one who is against you, the one who is complaining about the joy, the health, wealth and happiness that you have. The Psalmist prayed, "Rescue me from the mouth of the lions…" (Psalm 22:21). In the New Testament God says you can take steps to keep your head out of the lion's mouth.

I have a recording of a great comedian of a past era named Stanley Holloway. One of the wonderful monologues he gives on that record is about Albert, the son of Mr and Mrs Ramsbottom. They went to Blackpool for a holiday but there were not many exciting things to do or watch, so they decided to visit the zoo. Now Albert had always been told that lions were ferocious creatures; they would eat you up as soon as look at you. When they got to the zoo and looked in the lion's enclosure, there was Wallace the lion, lying down in front of the cage with his head just against the bars, and he appeared to be sleeping. Young Albert thought that this creature couldn't be a lion because it was not like the lion he had been told about. His Dad had with him a walking stick with a horse's head handle, and Albert took the stick and shoved it into Wallace's ear. Of course, the lion wasn't too happy about this and grabbed the stick with his mouth and pulled Albert into the cage and ate him. The poor mother said afterwards she felt a little down in the mouth, and her husband said, "Yes, and I think Albert does, too!"

The Bible describes the devil as a lion, a prowling, roaring lion, looking for someone to devour. Some translations state that he is a lion with a fierce hunger, so hungry that he will eat almost anything. However, there are ways that you can stop him, in fact, there are ways that you can so strengthen yourself in the Lord that you can almost forget that he is around. In the verses quoted above, I Peter 5:8-9, there are four "Be's", four keys to keeping yourself out of the lion's mouth.

Self-controlled

The first "Be" is Be Self-controlled (sober, KJV). It should come as no surprise that the Greek word translated "self-controlled" or "sober" means to be not intoxicated. This passage is not necessarily talking about alcohol, although perhaps that message is there for those who need it. When a driver of a car is not sober his reactions slow down, his concept of the physical world is altered and he does things he would not normally do. God says to us, "Be sober, be self-controlled, be aware with all your senses, totally sharp." Why should we do this? There is a lion roaming around, looking for someone to devour. This is an important key.

Some translations render the phrase as "stay well-balanced" or "exercise self-control". The moment you ease off a little, the moment you get into a state of euphoria created by wine or whatever, at that moment you have let your guard down and the devil sees the opportunity to get at you. I don't want to spend a lot of time on this key, but it is there in the New Testament and we must be aware of it. Be self-controlled. The battle today is for the mind of the believer. The devil will drop thoughts in your head that, as you look back on them, are toxic thoughts. These poisonous thoughts will lead you down the wrong track and straight into trouble. Be sober, be self-controlled.

Be alert

The second "Be" is Be Alert, be awake, be watchful, be vigilant. The price of freedom is eternal vigilance. Stay awake, keep your eyes open, be alert to what is happening around you. Drill into your mind the truth that God wants only health, wealth and happiness for you. When you do, you will sense something going wrong before there are outward signs of it. You know that certain things are not in God's will for your life. Stay awake, because if you miss the first sign then that thing might be upon you before you realise it. So stay sober and stay awake.

I like war movies, spy movies and detective movies. In many situations, maybe it is the underground in an occupied country or soldiers on patrol out in the woods, the characters are told to be alert, for their lives depend on being totally aware of every little thing that is happening around them. That's exactly what God is encouraging you to be here: Be Sober and Be Alert. In the previous chapter of I Peter these same two items appear together. "The end of all things is near. Therefore be clear minded and self-controlled so that you can pray" (I Peter 4:7). Be alert and sober. You can also find the two mentioned together in I Thessalonians, "So then, let us not be like others, who are asleep, but let us be alert and self-controlled" (I Thessalonians 5:6). So the first two "Be's" are powerful keys for you to use so you can be sure that the devil doesn't get your head in his mouth—be sober and be alert.

Withstand the devil

Then the passage tells us another step to take—Be Withstanding. Some translations use the word "resist" (NIV), but there is a difference between "resisting" and "withstanding". To resist something means that you are putting pressure against an object to endeavour to stop its forward movement. An example of this is weight training, which is based upon resistance, putting effort into resisting the weight caused by gravity. On the other hand, withstanding implies no active effort on your part at all, no striving, just standing firm. Let me illustrate it from the movie world. Imagine a solidly built bodyguard, standing with his arms folded, and the good guy comes up and punches him on the chin. The bodyguard just stands there as if it was only a fly that had brushed against his chin. I'm sure you have seen that situation many times. That is what the word "withstand" means.

There is no striving on your part, because you are never told to fight the devil. In Ephesians you are exhorted, "... do not give the devil a foothold" (Ephesians 4:27). In James you are again told to withstand him, "Submit yourselves, then, to God. Resist [withstand] the devil, and he will flee from you" (James 4:7). Now in I Peter you are told to "Withstand him..." (Weymouth). You are not told to fight a defeated foe, because the moment you start fighting him you agree with his viewpoint that he is not yet defeated. Your task is to withstand; I really think that is the best translation. To withstand the devil, just stand so firm that even if you feel some little bumps every now and again, you know where they are coming from. Yet you also know that God's strength within you is immeasurably stronger than the little bumps. "You, dear children, are from God and have overcome them, because the one who is in you is greater than the one who is in the world" (I John 4:4). That's why you can just give a "wink of faith", because you know it is not you but it is Christ living in you, the greater One. The devil may pound you and it's uncomfortable, but you can withstand his attacks. So Be Sober, Be Alert and Be Withstanding.

Stand firm in the faith

"Resist him, standing firm in the faith..." (I Peter 5:9a). "Keep your foothold in the faith" is how Moffat translates it. You stand firm because you have so drilled yourself in what you are in Christ that nothing can move you from it. Be "steadfast in the faith" (KJV), "firm in your faith" (Weymouth), "strong in the faith" (Goodspeed). "Standing firm" is a military term, used of "a body of heavy-armed infantry formed in ranks and files close and deep" (Kenneth Wuest). It implies something which cannot be easily pushed around. You are to stand so firm that nothing external can move you or get you to hesitate or doubt. You are what your believing is. Your whole life, your ability to withstand this roaring lion, is based on what you believe.

If I could sit down with you and talk about Christian matters, the first thing I would try to establish is what do you believe about God. Once I know that, I know where you are heading. Do you believe that God is the big policeman in the sky, the great unapproachable One, the One Who makes you sick because you need some discipline? Is that what you believe? If so, I know what troubles are coming down your road, but if you believe that God is a great, big, wonderful God, that He wants only the best for His children, then it's inconceivable that a God of love could make you sick; it's inconceivable that God could cause you any harm. Do you believe God is right there where you are or do you believe that He is somewhere up there beyond the clouds, even beyond the Milky Way? Where is God? God is in Christ, and Christ is in you, the expectation of glory (Colossians 1:27). What you believe determines who you are, so be sure you are standing firm in a faith based upon the Word of God, not a belief based on hearsay or tradition. Your "foothold in the faith" must be based upon what God says in His Word, and particularly what He says in the epistles to the churches, to New Testament people.

Hebrews chapter 11 has a clear record of people who stood "firm in the faith". "And without faith it is impossible to please God, because anyone who comes to him must believe that he exists and that he rewards those who earnestly seek him" (Hebrews 11:6). Note that a person "must believe that he exists", and without that belief we have no Christian basis for faith. We must believe that the invisible God exists and we must also believe that "he rewards those who earnestly seek Him". There is more than just saying, "I believe in God", as James points out. "You believe that there is one God. Good! Even the demons believe that—and shudder" (James 2:19).

Hebrews 11 continues by listing the multitude who lived by faith in an unseen God. "By faith Noah... by faith Abraham... by faith Jacob... by faith Joseph... by faith Moses", and then verse 13, "All these people were still living by faith when they died. They did not receive the things promised; they only saw them and welcomed them from a distance. And they admitted that they were aliens and strangers on earth." Now verse 32, "And what more shall I say? I do not have time to tell about Gideon, Barak, Samson, Jephthah, David, Samuel and the prophets, who through faith conquered kingdoms, administered justice, and gained what was promised; who shut the mouths of lions..." (Hebrews 11:32–33). Faith was a reality to those people. You may have heard the expression "Putting the Christians to the lions"; that's exactly what they did. If they wanted to get out of the arena they had to deny their faith. The greatest example has to be Daniel, of course, in the lion's den, because the lions just took one sniff of Daniel and said, "That boy is sanctified flesh and we're not going to touch him." Daniel stood firm in the faith.

In conclusion

Remember, you are victorious against all the onslaughts of your enemy, the devil. The four keys to doing this are: Be Sober, Be Vigilant, Be Withstanding and Be Standing Firm in the faith. This is not a negative subject but a very positive subject. The "Be's" are very positive—the subject is only negative if you fill your mind with the thought that the devil is going to get you. However, if you fill your mind with the truth that you are stronger than Satan, then it really doesn't matter what he tries to throw in your direction. Your faith will take care of it. The Bible clearly teaches it is the common lot of Christians to suffer persecution. But everyone likewise has the advantage of enjoying victory over the devil, for we are victorious ones, we are more than conquerors through Him that loved us.

Chapter Eight

How to Kill the Giants In Your Life

*G*iants have not always been giants. They started out as babies, just small, helpless things, little wonders, just like you and I started out life. There is a comparison here with the challenges you face. How often do you wonder whether such and such is going to work or not? The giants that eventually get you down start as a little "I wonder". You consider the problem, and as you do you find it growing, and before you know it your little thought of "I wonder" has become a doubt. And as you look at it a bit longer, it grows before your eyes and becomes a worry. And before you know it, you have a first-class anxiety on your mind. Now you really must give it your full attention, and before long it becomes an overwhelming fear, a very real giant in your life. Most of us have been down that road.

I clipped a report out of the newspaper some years ago, attributed to the London *Daily Mail*. It reports the death of Gem Gilbert, a British tennis star at the time. Years before, when she was a little girl, she had gone to the dentist with her mother. Her mother was to have a tooth extracted, and a most unusual and tragic thing happened. The little girl watched in horror as her mother died in the dentist's chair. She was terrified and her mind painted an indelible picture, to the extent that she related death to the dentist. She would not go near a dentist, but the day came when the pain in a tooth was so great that she agreed to have the dentist come to her house and take care of the tooth. She also wisely asked her minister to come along as well, as she needed support because of the fear that had developed over the years. So the minister was there and the dentist was there. The dentist unwrapped his bag of tools and as soon as she saw those tools, she collapsed and died. That is the power of fear.

Theodore Roosevelt said that the only thing we have to fear is fear itself. However, Christians have nothing to fear. We don't even have to fear fear itself if we believe the principles of God's Word. Someone else said that fear is sand in the machinery of life. Fear is like a can of worms. If you open a can of live worms, it is hard to get them back in the can because they seem to take up far more space than when they were in the can. Fear is just like that—the moment you open the can of fear, the moment you give it a thought, and thus give it power, it gets bigger and bigger and suddenly you have real problems.

David and the giant

Let's look at the record in the 17th chapter of the first book of Samuel and see how David took care of the giant Goliath, who generated fear. The two armies were camped on opposing sides of a valley, and every day for forty days, morning and night, Goliath came down into the valley. He looked at the Israelites, the people of God, and said, "Why don't you find yourself a man to come out and fight me?" And every morning and night the army of Israel turned around and ran back to their camp. There was plenty of fear in that situation!

We do not know how tall people were in those days, but we can assume that they were fairly average compared to what we are, perhaps even smaller. It is quite obvious that whatever height Goliath was, he was considerably bigger than they were. He didn't even have to jump to dunk a basketball! Commentators suggest he was around nine or ten feet tall (nearly 3 metres). So he was an enormous man and probably well proportioned to suit his height. Perhaps we can understand why there was nobody in the nation of Israel who was game to go out and fight him. Even the king was unable to entice his men to stand and fight. "'Do you see how this man keeps coming out? He comes out to defy Israel. The king will give great wealth to the man who kills him. He will also give him his daughter in marriage and will exempt his father's family from taxes in Israel.'" (I Samuel 17:25). I would have thought that exemption from taxes alone would have been great motivation!

David, who was too young to be a soldier, had been instructed by his father to take food to his brothers who were serving in the army. David met them and as they were exchanging greetings, "...Goliath, the Philistine champion from Gath, stepped out from his lines and shouted his usual defiance, and David heard it. When the Israelites saw the man, they all ran from him in great fear" (I Samuel 17:23a–24). There are two responses you can have to fear, and the army of Israel demonstrated one very graphically—run and hide. Now I don't know what I would have done if I had been there, but a very common response to fear is to run and hide.

David's response

However, David had different ideas and they were not the result of the impetuousness of youth (he was perhaps only 17 or 18 years old). "David asked the men standing near him, 'What will be done for the man who kills this Philistine and removes this disgrace from Israel? Who is this uncircumcised Philistine that he should defy the armies of the living God?'" (I Samuel 17:26). It was a disgrace that Israel's army, the same army that had won the battle of Jericho and had conquered the whole land of Israel, was now being held at bay by one heathen man. David's response was not to run and hide but to stand and change the situation. So there are two responses we can make to fear—you can run and hide and allow fear to dictate your life, or you can stand up and do something about it. The time to take action is when the giant is still a baby. Kill the giant when it's just an "I wonder", when it's just a little doubt—don't wait till he gets 10 foot high.

While there had been rewards offered for the defeat of Goliath, David was motivated more by the fact that it was a disgrace for the people of God to put up with this situation any longer. "What David said was overheard and reported to Saul, and Saul sent for him. David said to Saul, 'Let no one lose heart on account of this Philistine; your servant will go and fight him.' Saul replied, 'You are not able to go out against this Philistine and fight him; you are only a boy, and he has been a fighting man from his youth.' But David said to Saul, 'Your servant has been keeping his father's sheep. When a lion or a bear came and carried off a sheep from the flock, I went after it, struck it and rescued the sheep from its mouth. When it turned on me, I seized it by its hair, struck it and killed it. Your servant has killed both the lion and the bear; this uncircumcised Philistine will be like one of them, because he has defied the armies of the living God'" (I Samuel 17:31–36).

David's resources

To David the giant was no worse than a lion or a bear out in the wilderness. Was that the brashness of youth? No, because David gave the Lord credit for delivering him out of the paw of the lion and out of the paw of the bear (verse 37). David's resource was his faith in God. Saul gave him his blessing, but wanted David to wear his armour, so he put his helmet on David's head and put his armour around his body. David strapped Saul's sword around him but he now found he was no longer able to walk, so he took it all off.

David was happier with the resources with which he was acquainted. He took his shepherd's staff. He'd been out in the fields hundreds of times and he knew the value of having that staff in his hand. He also had a slingshot, so he took that also. To while away the time watching the flocks he had practised hitting objects, and no doubt he had used the slingshot to scare off wolves and bears. He got quite good at using it, for he was just a boy at heart. David was accustomed to these things, the normal equipment of a shepherd, and so he took his slingshot and his staff. It's an important point, because he was fighting the enemy with what he had. You see, so many say, "I could take care of that problem if only I had more money, or if only I had a bigger house, or if only I had a Mercedes, or if only..." Saul wanted him to go with the best material resources available, but David took care of the challenge with his faith in God and his faith in the familiar objects that he had.

"Then he took his staff in his hand, chose five smooth stones from the stream, put them in the pouch of his shepherd's bag and, with his sling in his hand, approached the Philistine. Meanwhile, the Philistine, with his shield bearer in front of him, kept coming closer to David" (I Samuel 17:40–41). Goliath, his enemy, had faith in his own strength, and in his familiar equipment—an enormous javelin, a spear with a heavy head on it, a large sword, and his own shield bearer who walked in front of him. Goliath was trusting in the strength of man and in his material resources. So not only are there two responses to fear, there are two kinds of resources for the fight. Next we shall see that there are also two reports, because there was a verbal battle before the real action started.

David's report

"He [Goliath] looked David over and saw that he was only a boy, ruddy and handsome, and he despised him. He said to David, 'Am I a dog, that you come at me with sticks?' And the Philistine cursed David by his gods. 'Come here,' he said, 'and I'll give your flesh to the birds of the air and the beasts of the field!'" (I Samuel 17:42-44). That is one-up-manship—psych out your enemy before you start the battle. Did it worry David? No, because David had his own one-up-manship. "David said to the Philistine, 'You come against me with sword and spear and javelin, but I come against you in the name of the Lord Almighty, the God of the armies of Israel, whom you have defied. This day the Lord will hand you over to me, and I'll strike you down and cut off your head. Today I will give the carcasses of the Philistine army to the birds of the air and the beasts of the earth, and the whole world will know that there is a God in Israel. All those gathered here will know that it is not by sword or spear that the Lord saves; for the battle is the Lord's, and he will give all of you into our hands.'" (I Samuel 17:45-47).

There are some quite good verbal pictures there. David pictured Goliath headless and then the vultures and wild animals taking care of the rest of the army, while Goliath pictured David as being dead and the vultures and wild animals taking care of the Israelites. So, is it equal? No, it's one of the most unequal of contests in history—"for the battle is the Lord's". David spoke words of faith, he really believed what he said. In fact, I think he could even picture in his mind Goliath's big head lying there on the ground separated from the body. David was totally convinced of it. He spoke the word of faith and he expected it to come to pass. Then he took the step of faith, and it had to be a step of faith to face a 10-

foot man with all his equally large equipment. It's an incredible step of faith but it's worth taking, because the step of faith backs up the word of faith, and faith produces the answer.

David's step of faith

David reached into his bag and took out a stone. He put it in his slingshot, fired it and it hit the Philistine in his forehead. The stone sank into his forehead and he fell on his face (verse 49). There's no truth in the story that a very old manuscript says that while Goliath was on his way down he was heard to say, "A thing like that never entered my head before!" Just one little stone and down went Goliath. David didn't need swords or spears or shields, he just needed to speak a word of faith and to take a step of faith. He believed that one little stone would find its mark on the very spot that would bring the giant down to a workable size.

"So David triumphed over the Philistine with a sling and a stone; without a sword in his hand he struck down the Philistine and killed him. David ran and stood over him. He took hold of the Philistine's sword and drew it from the scabbard. After he killed him, he cut off his head with the sword. When the Philistines saw that their hero was dead, they turned and ran" (I Samuel 17:50–51). When David finally got the giant to the ground he finished the rest of his prophetic word of faith. He took Goliath's sword, killed him and then cut off his head.

What can we learn from this record? Fear, if you allow it, will grow up into a giant. Like you, I have a most active mind and if my wife is late coming home from shopping, my mind starts racing immediately and thinking all the dreadful things that could have happened. The time to slay the giant is right then when the first doubt hits the mind. Slay that giant by remembering that fear is opposed to what God says about you. God says that your entitlement is health, wealth and happiness. Fear says you are not going to be healthy, or wealthy but miserable. Since those thoughts are opposed to the knowledge of God, you slay them. You take your stand, speak the word of faith and get that giant of fear down to size.

So the story of David and Goliath really teaches principles of how to kill the giants in your life. You can either run or you can stand. Remember, all giants start their lives as babies, and that's the time to deal with them.

Chapter Nine

How to Handle Discouragement

*A*ll of us seem to get into situations where it is easy to become discouraged, despondent, or depressed. If we had a full appreciation of what God has done in and for us, then perhaps we would not get discouraged. However, until we come to a total belief of the totality of His work in us, there will be days when it is easy to get discouraged. There has to be a way to break this cycle and I believe the best answer is the Bible answer.

In my research I found many Bible examples of discouragement, including several involving the nation of Israel. When they were delivered out of the bondage of Egypt and were on their wilderness wanderings, the record says, "And the soul of the people was much discouraged [impatient, NIV] because of the way" (Numbers 21:4 KJV). When Nehemiah brought the nation back from Babylon and they had the task of rebuilding the walls, they became very discouraged because there was just so much rubble to move that they couldn't get on with the task (Nehemiah 4:10). Many individuals in the Bible also got discouraged, such as Moses, David, Elijah, even the disciples of Jesus. I have chosen Elijah as a good, representative example, and one from which we can learn the secret to handling discouragement.

Let me give the background to the record in I Kings chapter 19. In the previous chapter, Elijah had confronted the 850 false prophets of Baal. They were paid for out of the nation's treasury and someone has estimated that if they had been paid only $15 a week there was an outgo of over $660,000 a year to false prophets by a nation which was supposed to be God's chosen people. That was quite a drain on the budget! However, God and Elijah made a majority over the 850 false prophets, and when they failed to bring down fire from heaven on to a sacrificial altar, Elijah saw to it that they all were killed.

Then Jezebel, the queen, heard what Elijah had done. "So Jezebel sent a messenger to Elijah to say, 'May the gods deal with me, be it ever so severely, if by this time tomorrow I do not make your life like that of one of them.'" (I Kings 19:2 NIV). Elijah had reduced the budget deficit but the queen was not impressed! When he received her message, "Elijah was afraid and ran for his life. When he came to Beersheba in Judah, he left his servant there, while he himself went a day's journey into the desert. He came to a broom tree, sat down under it and prayed that he might die. 'I have had enough, Lord,' he said. 'Take my life; I am no better than my ancestors.'" (I Kings 19:3-4).

I do not know why Elijah did not take a stand like he had with the false prophets of Baal. As the record proceeds we discover that he was very depressed. He ran into the wilderness with his servant and then told his servant to stay while he went on a further day's journey into the desert. He did that so that even his servant wouldn't know where he was if Jezebel should come looking for him. He found a broom or juniper tree and sat down in the shade of the tree. Elijah wanted God to end his life—that's real depression, isn't it?

There are a lot of depressed Christians sitting under juniper trees, under bushes in the desert. I do not want to see you sitting there for long, so let's see what happened next.

God's support is available

"Then he lay down under the tree and fell asleep" (I Kings 19:5a). Right there, in the midst of Elijah's depression, God demonstrated His support by sending an angel to look after him. Angels have a definite part in God's plan. The New Testament calls them ministering spirits, "Are not all angels ministering spirits sent to serve those who will inherit salvation?" (Hebrews 1:14). In the Old Testament, the Psalmist said, "For he will command his angels concerning you to guard you in all your ways" (Psalm 91:11). God's support is constant. Not only has God placed Christ within us and given us the power to handle every situation that we could ever run across, but also He has His angels around us, specifically instructed to look after you and me. That is tremendous!

When you get to that tight spot in life when you feel you just can't go on, then remember that God's support is right there. You don't need to wait until 11 a.m. Sunday morning, you don't even need to pick up the phone and call the minister. God's support is right there the moment you need it. What was Elijah doing from the moment he heard of Jezebel's challenge to when he sat down under the juniper tree? He was running—run, run, run. One of Satan's favourite tricks is to get you so busy that you don't have time to listen to God. I love that verse that says, "Be still, and know that I am God" (Psalm 46:10). When you get still, you can hear God's voice and make yourself aware of His presence. Elijah did not hear God because he was too busy running away from Jezebel, too busy turning his head to see who was following. Only when he got quiet could God get through to him.

So remember, God's support is always available when you feel down, when you feel discouraged. God cares for you. He knows what you need. He knows what you are going through. In fact, He even knows how it's going to turn out. So relax and enjoy God's support. Elijah sat down under the tree, probably exhausted, and he slept.

God's supply is available

Then what happened? "All at once an angel touched him and said, 'Get up and eat' He looked around, and there by his head was a cake of bread baked over hot coals, and a jar of water. He ate and drank and then lay down again. The angel of the Lord came back a second time and touched him and said, 'Get up and eat, for the journey is too much for you.' So he got up and ate and drank" (I Kings 19:5b–8a).

We should not be surprised that God's supply was available to Elijah, because God knew what he needed. God knows that you need health, so He has made health available to you by His spirit within you, a healthy spirit. God knows that you need wealth, so He has made wealth available to you. God knows that you need happiness, so He has made happiness available to you. God knows what you need! Much of the discouragement we feel is because our desires have not been fulfilled according to our timetable. We think this and that should have happened by now.

David, the psalmist, became so discouraged that he complained to God, "My tears have been my food day and night, while men say to me all day long, 'Where is your God?' (Psalms 42:3). He was asking, "Where are you, God?" Yet God was right there with him. That's where He always is and that's where you will discover the answer that supplies your need.

Elijah found this, too. It was quite amazing—lying asleep under a tree in the middle of the desert and waking up to find his favourite angel's food cake and a jar of water at his head. Now that's room service! That is how our God looks after His family. The angel encouraged him to eat, so he ate so much that he fell asleep again. The angel of the Lord woke him up again and told him to eat some more. God's support was right there when he needed it. God's supply was there to build him up again so he could do what God wanted him to do. He could now go forth and make a success out of the rest of his life.

I believe there is some symbolism in the cake of bread and the jar of water. The bread to me symbolises the Word of God. "Man does not live on bread alone, but on every word that comes from the mouth of God" (Matthew 4:4). When you feel down and discouraged, the best thing you can do is to get into God's Word and read some of those powerful, positive, divine promises that are recorded there. Get some of God's thoughts flowing through your mind. You became discouraged because of Satan's thoughts flowing through your mind. Get God's thoughts in there by feeding on His Word and you will see the situation change dramatically.

The water symbolises the spirit of God within you. Jesus said, "But whoever drinks the water I give him will never thirst. Indeed, the water I give him will become in him a spring of water welling up to eternal life" (John 4:14). And later He said, "'Whoever believes in me, as the Scripture has said, streams of living water will flow from within him.' By this he meant the Spirit, whom those who believed in him were later to receive. Up to that time the Spirit had not been given, since Jesus had not yet been glorified" (John 7:38–39).

The spirit of God within you is a perpetual spring of water, bringing life and growth to wherever it is applied. As you are a Christian, you have that spirit, a perpetual spring bubbling away whether you are on top of the world or sitting discouraged under a juniper tree. The perpetual spring still flows—you must simply recognise it is there, tap into it and enjoy its benefits. So God's supply was two-fold: the cake of bread and the water. God's supply to you is the Word of God and the spirit of God within you. You need both. If you rely only on the Word and not the spirit, then you will just have Bible knowledge, head knowledge, which of itself will not necessarily help you through all of life's situations. If you rely only on the spirit within, you have zeal without knowledge, and that can be dangerous. But if you rely on the combination of the two—God's Word and the living spirit within you that makes that Word come alive—then you are well on the way to recovery from discouragement.

God's strength is available

I want to show you one further truth. "So he got up and ate and drank. Strengthened by that food, he travelled forty days and forty nights until he reached Horeb, the mountain of God" (I Kings 19:8b). That was quite some meal, wasn't it? It beats a lot of diets I've heard about—one meal and you can walk forty days and forty nights! When Elijah got quiet, he recognised God's support and partook of God's supply, then he could go forth in God's strength. He manifested the strength that was within. As you increase your awareness of the dynamic strength that God has placed within you, you can handle situations that previously would have resulted in discouragement, despondency, or depression.

I can remember the first time I flew around the world. I had to stay over in Singapore because my flight had been delayed and I missed the connection to Australia. On the next day I went into the airline office to confirm my ongoing flight. They checked my passport and changed my ticket for the flight. Then they wanted to see my health certificate—this was in the days when countries were very particular about smallpox and cholera inoculations. I only had an inoculation for smallpox and I had come from Israel and been in transit through Tehran and Bombay. However, there had been a cholera outbreak in Tehran and I was told that Australia would not let me in without a cholera injection. As I was just understanding some of the truth about God's power and health in my life, I refused to have it. So they allowed me to board the flight only if I signed a declaration that if Australia refused me entry then they would carry me on to their next destination (Fiji) at my expense. I signed the form and boarded the plane.

I had the most depressing flight that I've ever had! Even though at the time the airlines went out of their way to give you the best, even in economy class, I was just miserable. I spent most of the time trying to think of all the ways that I could get around what I thought would happen when I landed in Perth, Western Australia. I considered that if one preacher friend of mine was there to meet me, all would be well, for he could talk the hind leg off a donkey! Have you ever been in a situation like that? However, I finally came to the conclusion that I was a man of God doing God's work, and I also knew I had an Australian passport which gave me an absolute right to enter the country. I was not about to let any little "god" in the health department stop me.

When I got off the plane at the Perth airport, I waved to my wife and children through the glass divider and went through immigration. The officer stamped my passport and then he opened up my health card, thumbed through all 24 pages and all he found was a record of a smallpox inoculation. He asked me where I had been and I said, "I have come from Israel and I've been in transit through Tehran, Bombay and Singapore." When he heard that, he stamped the health card and sent me through. I had spoiled a good flight because I got depressed about the situation. However, finally my faith had won through, because I was victorious in that situation.

Elijah knew that he could go forth in the strength of God. He walked for forty days and forty nights to Horeb, the mountain of God, and then received a new revelation from God. Your strength comes from knowing who you are as well as knowing Who is in you. Who are you? "Oh, I'm just a human." No, you're not; you are a son or daughter of God. You have God's seed in you (I John 3:9). Christ is in you (Galatians 2:20). You and God are a majority. There is not any situation that you and God cannot handle together, if you will go about it God's way. "My grace is sufficient for you, for my power is made perfect in weakness" (II Corinthians 12:9). When you come to the end of your resources, that is the time when you must increase your awareness of the truth that God is available to help you through.

How do you handle discouragement, despondency, or depression? By getting quiet enough to recognise that God's support is always with you, God's supply is on hand when you need it and God's strength will carry you through every situation in life.

Chapter Ten

How to Survive a Catastrophe

There are plenty of catastrophes in the world this week. People are dying in civil wars, there are areas with great famine, earthquakes, plane crashes, in fact, there are so many that a half-hour news service cannot seem to fit them all in.

On top of all this are those personal catastrophes that folk seem to have. Some folk lose their jobs and think it is a catastrophe rather than seeing it as a stepping stone to something better. Perhaps others have been in a car accident and they think it is a catastrophe because the paintwork was scratched. I can remember the night I thought it was a catastrophe when I couldn't work out Rubik's cube! We all have experiences that to us are catastrophes and we need to learn how to survive those experiences of life, those tight spots where things are difficult. Actually the word "catastrophe" is a Greek word that appears in the Bible. It is derived from two Greek words, *cata* meaning "down" and *strophe* meaning "to turn", a downturn. We might say that the economy has suffered a downturn, and so we have a catastrophe on our hands.

By way of introduction I will quote just two verses that use the Greek word "catastrophe". "Jesus... overturned the tables of the money changers and the benches of those selling doves" (Matthew 21:12 NIV). The word for "overthrow" is the word "catastrophe". For the money-changers it was a catastrophe! It is also used in the New Testament concerning false teaching, how it overthrows the faith of believers. "... Quarreling about words... only ruins those who listen" (II Timothy 2:14). The word for "ruins" is the word "catastrophe". False teaching is a catastrophe to those who listen to it and believe it. To learn how to set the stage in order to survive a catastrophe, I will share with you an Old Testament record.

Noah is a good example of a man who survived a catastrophe. Genesis chapter 6 tells us of the conditions that were on the earth at the time of Noah. "The Lord saw how great man's wickedness on the earth had become, and that every inclination of the thoughts of his heart was only evil all the time... Now the earth was corrupt in God's sight and was full of violence" (Genesis 6:5,11). Does that sound to you just like today? It certainly does! Jesus commented on it when He said, "For in the days before the flood, people were eating and drinking, marrying and giving in marriage, up to the day Noah entered the ark and they knew nothing about what would happen until the flood came and took them all away. That is how it will be at the coming of the Son of Man" (Matthew 24:38–39). I think this proves again the point that the Bible is intensely relevant and practical, because we have not changed much in spite of our sophistication with all our gadgets and computerisation.

There are four statements concerning Noah that will teach us how to set the stage in order to survive a catastrophe. "The Lord was grieved that he had made man on the earth, and his heart was filled with pain. So the Lord said, 'I will wipe mankind, whom I have created, from the face of the earth—men and animals, and creatures that move along the ground, and birds of the air—for I am grieved that I have made them.' But Noah found favour in the eyes of the Lord" (Genesis 6:6–8). If you were living on the earth in those days, you would have thought that a catastrophe was coming. "But...", and notice the strength of that word in verse 8, "Noah found favour (grace, KJV) in the eyes of the Lord." Then verse 9 amplifies the statement, "This is the account of Noah. Noah was a righteous man, blameless among the people of his time, and he walked with God" (Genesis 6:9).

Noah found grace

That is why Noah survived the catastrophe, the same reason why you can survive anything that the world throws at you—you have found grace in the eyes of the Lord. Remember, Noah lived in Old Testament times even before the ten commandments had been given, so there were no requirement to fulfil any ritual as later developed in the Jewish religion. Noah was a man who did the best he could, and in the administration that he was under God required people to live a blameless life. Today you can live a good life and still miss heaven because God's administration has changed. Noah was not one of those whose "every inclination of the thoughts of his heart was only evil all the time". He was a righteous man and blameless among the people of his time. So it was because of his righteous works that Noah found grace in the eyes of the Lord.

I'm glad that today the situation is different for you and me, "For it is by grace you have been saved, through faith—and this not from yourselves, it is the gift of God—not by works, so that no one can boast" (Ephesians 2:8–9). I'm thrilled that everybody in the family of God can survive any catastrophe because we have found grace in the eyes of the Lord. We have found it in a different way from how Noah found it, but we found it, nevertheless. In fact, as you study your Bible you will find that we have a far better deal than Noah ever had.

Noah walked with God

Noah not only found grace in the eyes of the Lord, but in verse 9 it says that Noah "walked with God". This statement implies a continuous walk and a close relationship. One of my favourite gospel songs says, "The King and I walk hand in hand together…" The chorus of another old gospel hymn says, "And He walks with me and He talks with me, and He tells me I am His own, and the joy we share as we tarry there none other has ever known." That is the relationship Noah had with God. He had a moment-by-moment walk with God. Because of this relationship, God told him of events that were about to happen. "So God said to Noah, 'I am going to put an end to all people, for the earth is filled with violence because of them. I am surely going to destroy both them and the earth'." (Genesis 6:13). God let Noah in on what was going to happen. The Lord God Who created heaven and earth had a one-to-one relationship with Noah.

How do you walk with someone who is totally unseen? Hebrews 11 tells us what was Noah's secret. "By faith Noah, when warned about things not yet seen, in holy fear built an ark to save his family. By his faith he condemned the world and became heir of the righteousness that comes by faith" (Hebrews 11:7). It is by faith that you and I walk with someone we cannot see. It's the faith walk that will help you survive a catastrophe. God calls things that are not as though they were (Romans 4:17). You will need to do as God does in order to survive a catastrophe. You will need to declare that the situation is going to change. You will need to see things not as they are, but as they are going to become. It was by faith that Noah and God walked together hand in hand, and it is by faith that you and God do the same.

Noah did all God commanded him

"So make yourself an ark of cypress wood; make rooms in it and coat it with pitch inside and out" (Genesis 6:14). "Noah did everything just as God commanded him" (Genesis 6:22). "And Noah did all that the Lord commanded him" (Genesis 7:5).

There is a progression in these statements concerning Noah. He found grace in the eyes of the Lord, he walked with God, and he did all that the Lord commanded him. God requires the same from you. He wants you to find grace and he wants you to walk with Him on a moment-by-moment basis, and then He wants you to do all that He has commanded you. I have a record of comedian Bill Cosby telling the story of Noah. He imagines Noah building the ark in his driveway and how all the neighbours made their unkind comments as he went to work. Whenever Noah got frustrated and said he was not going to go along with this crazy idea anymore, God had to remind him, "Noah, can you tread water?" Yes, you too might get frustrated at times yet you must still do all that God has commanded you to do. When you do that, the responsibility is on God for your survival, not on your own shoulders.

So Noah built the ark and then somehow coaxed into it a pair of each unclean animal and seven pairs of each clean animal. That was an interesting experience! Many of us in Australia wonder why he didn't swat the mosquitoes while he had the two of them handy and he could have also swatted a couple of house flies while he was about it. It could have made our lives a lot easier! The ark floated when the rains came down and Noah was in the ark one year and 17 days. That was quite a journey! Now we come to the fourth statement concerning Noah.

Noah thanked God

"Then Noah built an altar to the LORD and, taking some of all the clean animals and clean birds, he sacrificed burnt offerings on it" (Genesis 8:20). You might wonder why he offered clean animals. If you read the whole record you would discover that Noah took in seven pairs of all the clean animals and only one pair of the unclean animals (God told him how to tell the difference). There were enough pairs of clean animals so that he could take some to make a sacrifice of thanksgiving to God, a sacrifice that said, "Thank you, Lord, for getting us through that catastrophe." Worship can precede and follow blessing. The moment Noah had the opportunity, soon after the ark rested on top of Mount Ararat, he stepped off the ark and found that the ground was dry. He then collected some wood and built an altar and worshipped his God.

You can learn something from that, I'm sure. Now that you have found grace in the eyes of the Lord, and have the opportunity every day to walk with God and to do all the Lord has commanded you to do, you too should be thanking God. You can do this every day! Don't wait for a catastrophe to loom on the horizon and don't wait to see results before you offer a sacrifice of thanksgiving. If you are about to go into a business, thank the Lord for the right location with the right facilities at the right price for all your activities. For your own personal life, thank the Lord for health in your body, for taking care of that account, for this and for that. Offer the sacrifice of thanksgiving.

After Noah thanked the Lord, the record says, "Then God blessed Noah and his sons, saying to them, 'Be fruitful and increase in number and fill the earth'." (Genesis 9:1). God blessed Noah and his sons. Worship precedes blessing. God looked after Noah through the catastrophe and then God said, "Now it's up to you, Noah. Go out and make it work." One of the first prosperity statements in the Bible is in this verse: "Be fruitful and increase." Noah got busy and he enjoyed life while he was doing it. In addition, God took care of Noah's future. "I have set my rainbow in the clouds... Never again will the waters become a flood to destroy all life... This is the sign of the covenant I have established between me and all life on the earth" (Genesis 9:13,15,17).

In conclusion

So that is the record of how Noah set the stage in order to survive a catastrophe. The record is written so that you can see that it is possible for you to survive anything that this world might throw at you. Let me say, however, that I do not believe we should go around with the attitude of wondering what is going to happen next. If you expect disaster you will get what you expect. You should be expecting only good in your life. Because all of life is an ebb and a flow, there do come times when it will look to you from your limited, finite viewpoint that you are about to be swamped by a catastrophe. Later on, years later, when you look back on it, you may well see it as just a silly little incident not worth mentioning in your life story. However, when you are in the middle of the challenge it may well look to you like a catastrophe. At that time remember that you can survive the catastrophe because you are on God's team, the team of grace—Great Riches At Christ's Expense. You can walk with God, you can obey God, you can offer thanksgiving to God. I recall an old Negro spiritual that says, "Noah found grace in the eyes of the Lord, and he landed high and dry". He survived, and you can too!

Last Words

*O*ur time together has come to a close. I have enjoyed sharing these truths with you, and will enjoy it even more when you write and tell me how this book has helped you.

Read this book again. You will be surprised at how much more you retain after a second reading. Look up the Bible verses in other translations and soak your mind in these practical truths from the positive Word of God.

Give out copies of this book to your family, friends and fellowship—start a stream of blessing! And write today; I look forward to receiving your letter.

GPO Box 450, Adelaide SA 5001, Australia